THE BIG WEEK OF WORLD WAR II

"I could see the omen of the war's end when I lay in my sick bed and watched the bombers of the American Fifteenth Air Force fly across the Alps from their Italian bases to bomb German industrial targets and there wasn't a German fighter plane anywhere in sight."

—Albert Speer

There could be no better testimonial to the success of the Big Week campaign . . . probably the most decisive battle in the history of aerial warfare.

BIG WEEK!

by
Glenn Infield

PINNACLE BOOKS • NEW YORK CITY

To Bill
A bombardier who didn't return

BIG WEEK!

An original Pinnacle Books edition, published for the
first time anywhere.

ISBN: 0-523-00285-8

Photo credits: Courtesy of the author's private collection,
the U.S. Air Force, and Wide World Photos, Inc.

First printing, January 1974

Printed in the United States of America

PINNACLE BOOKS, INC.
275 Madison Avenue
New York, N.Y. 10016

ACKNOWLEDGMENTS

The material for this book was obtained by interviews with individuals involved with air combat in the European theater of war before, during, and after Big Week; by studying official documents at the USAF Archives, Maxwell Air Force Base, Alabama; researching material available at the Imperial War Museum, London; checking Luftwaffe records at Freiburg, West Germany and Berlin; and reading unit histories, papers, personal accounts, and various other valuable documents provided me by numerous individuals and organizations that were interested in having the story of Big Week told accurately.

Rose B. Coombs, librarian, Imperial War Museum; Marguerite Kennedy, Chief, Archives Branch of the USAF Historical Research Division; General James H. Doolittle; General Ira C. Eaker; General Thomas S. Jeffrey, Jr.; Hans-Joachim Kroschinski, Karl Ries, and Kowalewski, all of West Germany; and a host of others too numerous to mention but well aware of the invaluable aid they gave me during the writing of this book deserve more appreciation than these few words can offer. I am particularly grateful to the former Luftwaffe pilots who were so generous with their time and information when I visited Germany and who greeted me as a friend even when they learned that I had been their enemy during Big Week. While this is not a personal account of the February 20–February 25, 1944, American heavy bomber missions over Germany, I did fly several of the missions as a pilot of a B-17 with the Ninety-fifth Bombardment Group (H) of the Eighth Air Force, and it was impossible not to include many of my own impressions in the book. In general, however, this is the story of the high-ranking American officers who planned Big Week, the American airmen and officers who flew the missions, and the Luftwaffe personnel who tried to destroy the Eighth Air Force during the violent air battles. To them I acknowledge my debt of gratitude.

CONTENTS

PREFACE

One of the most important periods in the history of aerial warfare, the six days of the European theater of operations air battles between February 20 and February 25, 1944, is known as Big Week. Some military experts compare it to the Battle of the Bulge and D-Day, among the greatest combat actions of World War II. Upon the outcome of these aerial battles depended the future of daylight precision bombing and the success or failure of the cross-Channel invasion scheduled for the spring of 1944. Ultimately the outcome of World War II depended on the results of the invasion, so Big Week played a vital role in the winning of the war by the Allies.

Before an invasion of the Continent by the Allied ground troops could be successful, the USAAF had to accomplish two objectives: The German factories producing their fighters had to be destroyed; and the Luftwaffe had to be destroyed in the air. As General H. H. Arnold said on December 27, 1943: "It is a conceded fact that Overlord [invasion] will not be possible unless the German Air Force is destroyed." Consequently, in February, 1944, the airman and officers of the USAAF set out to achieve the two objectives. This is the story of how they accomplished the assignment.

1
THE BRIEFING

Ninety-Fifth Bomb Group, England; 20 February, 1944 ...

The flashlight beam shooting out in the pitch blackness of the barracks hit Gene Manson flush in the eyes and seemed to set off an explosion in his brain. A hand shook his shoulder.

"Briefing at 0430."

The light moved on down the row of beds, stopping every now and then as the CQ repeated his message.

"How's the weather?" Manson called from his bed just before the CQ went out the door at the far end of the barracks.

"Clouds down to the roof," the CQ yelled and slammed the door on his way out.

Reluctantly Manson swung his feet out from under the blankets and sat on the edge of the bed a moment, trying to get his longjohns straightened out. Across the aisle a navigator, Mel Fladeboe, stood on top of his bed and sang a Norwegian folk song as was his custom before every mission.

"Shut up," someone cried. "You make me sick."

Fladeboe, however, kept on singing as though he hadn't heard the criticism.

His critic gave up with a disgusted, "He'll sing himself right into hell."

Today could be the day, Manson decided, as he pulled on his pants. Not that a pilot or his crew didn't have a good chance of turning in his flying suit for a pair of wings in heaven or a shovel in hell on every mission, but today, February 20, 1944, the odds had jumped considerably. The wrong way!

Fully dressed, Manson grabbed his leather flying jacket, walked out into the blackness of the early morning and groped his way to the truck waiting to take the crews to the mess hall. He climbed into the truck, squeezed into an opening on the bench at the left side of the truck and tried to bury himself in his flight jacket to keep warm.

At the mess hall the eggs were fresh, not powdered. That meant trouble.

"The condemned man eats a hearty breakfast," a tail-gunner said quietly as he sat down at a table with his tray.

"Eat and be merry for tomorrow you die," another gunner wisecracked. Nobody laughed.

"Tomorrow, hell. Today."

Fresh eggs meant that the mission was going to be a rough one. The eggs were a treat, a bribe, something to remember when the wing caught fire and the doomed bomber dove earthward over enemy territory. Powdered eggs: a milk run. Fresh eggs: the red string on the map will be long.

Suddenly Manson wasn't hungry.

Half an hour later, he and the other crew members were checked by two sentries at the door of a blacked-out building, and finally, after passing the check, they stumbled into the glaring lights of the briefing room. Men were stretched out everywhere—some slumped in their chairs, some sitting stiffly upright on the edge of their seats, staring hypnotically at the covered map at the front of the room.

At exactly 0430 the roll was called by a second lieutenant, each plane commander answering for his entire crew. When the roll call was finished a slim, immaculately dressed lieutenant colonel, hair neatly combed and face

12

freshly shaven, mounted the raised platform and stood by the covered map. Within seconds the room became very still. All eyes watched as Lieutenant Colonel Harry Mumford, Group Operations Officer for the Ninety-Fifth Bombardment Group, reached over and pulled back the curtain concealing the map on the wall.

Every head followed the red lines on the map. One line went from England, across the English Channel, through Belgium, into Germany and on and on until at Leipzig it circled and headed back. Another line went north, across the North Sea, past Helgoland, across Denmark, and circled Rostock on a line almost directly north of Leipzig. No one spoke for a long time. A very long time. Then a gunner whistled softly and said, "I wish the chickens had kept their damn eggs. This ride is worth more than fresh eggs."

Others in the room began to talk. The room buzzed with excitement and bitching and wisecracks until Mumford broke it up.

"Today we go deep for the first time in clear weather since the Schweinfurt raid. Some of you were on that one and you know what to expect. The rest of you will find out. If we're lucky, it may just be a long trip. If we're not lucky, we are going to have one hell of a fight on our hands."

He took a pointer and traced the northern line. "The Ninety-Fifth will go to Rostock. We will have *no* fighter escort!"

The men sat stunned. No fighter escort? Even on the milk runs to the French coast the "little friends" were always along, circling and doing wingovers around the bomber boxes. No fighter escort? It would be suicide. . . .

So began Big Week, the aerial combat saga of World War II that has been compared to the Battle of the Bulge and D-Day as one of the greatest military actions of the entire conflict. There were not enough heavy bombers, not enough long-range fighters, not enough skilled crews ... but there was a vital need for the American bombers to break the back of German air power and clear the skies over Europe for the invasion. On February 20, 1944, the Ninety-Fifth Bombardment Group of the Eighth Air Force, joined by the other units of the Eighth Air Force and Fifteenth Air Force, based in Italy, took off to accomplish the assignment and for six days this great and decisive air battle was fought all over Western Europe, from the Zuider Zee to the Danube. . . .

2
THE PLAN

The most important period in the history of aerial warfare, the six days of the European theater of operations air battles between February 20 and 25, 1944, known as Big Week, was the culmination of events that began with an overall plan to defeat the Luftwaffe. This plan, designated AWPD-42 (Air War Plans Division, Air Staff, 1942) seemed clear and decisive, a blueprint for ultimate success. AWPD-42 was actually the reaffirmation of an earlier official USAAF position that had been outlined in September, 1941, a reaffirmation requested by President Franklin D. Roosevelt a year later when he was reviewing the requirements of the Army and Navy and of US production in order to have "complete ascendancy over the enemy." Colonel Harold L. George, Lieutenant Colonel Kenneth N. Walker, and Majors Laurence S. Kuter and Haywood S. Hansell had put together AWPD-1 for General H.H. Arnold, Commanding General of the Army Air Forces (at that time a major general and Chief of the Air Corps). And the strategic concepts drawn up by these young officers prior to Pearl Harbor were still valid in September, 1942, when AWPD-42 was issued.

It was obvious that the USAAF could not sustain an effective air offensive simultaneously against both Germany and Japan with the resources available; and when the choice was made, Germany was favored as the objective of first priority. There were several reasons for this decision: Foremost was the fact that air power alone could be brought directly to bear against Hitler's stronghold even during the period that Allied ground forces were unable to challenge the Axis ground forces on the Continent. If the Allied air forces, especially the USAAF, could deplete the Luftwaffe and destroy the economic structure that supported Hitler's land forces, an invasion of the Continent would be possible when the Allied ground forces reached the desired strength. Consequently at the Casablanca conference in January, 1943, a projected air offensive against Germany was approved by both the British and the Americans.

The American air offensive was aimed at 177 selected industrial or military targets grouped in seven categories which, Arnold said, if eliminated would deprive Hitler of the means to wage war. The seven categories, all listed in APWD-42 were:

1. German aircraft plants
2. Submarine yards
3. Transportation
4. Electric power
5. Oil
6. Aluminum
7. Rubber

Arnold estimated that the seven sources of Hitler's warmaking power could be reduced to helplessness with 133,000 tons of bombs delivered in approximately 66,000 sorties over a period of a few months. A more detailed breakdown of the plan indicated that a third of the targets were to be eliminated by the end of 1943 while the USAAF was being built up to its projected full strength, and the remainder of the targets destroyed during the first four months of 1944. Since the month of May, the deadline, would bring favorable tides and water conditions along the Normandy coast, the proposed invasion of the Continent by the Allied ground forces was tentatively set for that month. If it took the USAAF longer to complete the assignment, the invasion would be in jeopardy because it was imperative that the skies over Europe be controlled by Allied air power if such an invasion were to be successful. Unfortunately the guidelines and deadlines set by Arnold were not as realistic as they appeared to be at the time. Nor did the Luftwaffe have any intention of allowing the USAAF to accomplish the assignment.

It soon became obvious that it was not enough for the USAAF just to outline its strategy and set a deadline. It was also a necessity to secure the means with which to operate, and this meant obtaining aircraft—a large number of aircraft. The 1942 production goal had been 60,000 planes, of which slightly less than 40,000 were earmarked for the USAAF. This goal was not met. As the new year approached, it was clear that more aircraft would be needed in 1943 than had been asked for in 1942. The authors of AWPD-42 tried to predict the number of aircraft that would be required to destroy the 177 targets, basing their prediction on the bomb tonnage required and the sorties it would take to drop the estimated tonnage. Assuming that under European weather conditions five or six operations per month could be scheduled and using a British attrition rate of twenty percent a month, they decided that a USAAF bomber force of 2,965 heavy bombers were needed. If this force could be operational in the European theater of operations by January 1, 1944, it was thought that the proposed invasion of the Continent could be made on schedule in May.

The goals of AWPD-42 were opposed from the start by the US Navy, which decided that the USAAF was destined to get too large a share of the total production of 139,190 aircraft for 1943 when the planes needed in other theaters of war were considered, too. The US Navy rejected the plan in its entirety but the War Department General Staff and President Roosevelt agreed with the USAAF request, and it appeared that the strategic air offensive against Germany as planned by the AWPD-42 was set.

It wasn't!

It was one thing to request a total of 139,190 aircraft be built in 1943 but entirely another to accomplish the task when the required resources were not available. Donald M. Nelson, chairman of the War Production Board, immediately notified the War Department that the objective was completely out of line with the available production capacity of the nation. Even if the "must" items listed by President Roosevelt, such as the aircraft, the merchant ships, combat vessels, material plants, and Lend-Lease to the Soviet Union, were the only objectives considered, it was doubtful that they could be attained. This, of course, meant that many other essential items for war—but not on the "must" list—would not be produced until 1944. On October 29, 1942, after studying Nelson's message, President Roosevelt reduced the number of aircraft to be built in 1943 from the former figure of 139,190 to 107,-000 but insisted that this objective "be given the highest priority and whatever preference is needed to insure its accomplishment."

This was the first alteration in AWPD-42 that eventually led directly to Big Week more than a year later!

Not only did Arnold and his USAAF staff have to maintain continual pressure on the War Department to obtain the necessary bombers in 1943 to meet the first objective of AWPD-42—to destroy a third of the 177 selected targets by the end of the year—but they also had to prove to the British that daylight precision bombing was possible and practical. The British bombing doctrine was based on the assumption that "mass" or "area" attacks that would destroy industrial areas and workers' homes would ultimately cause a manpower shortage and weaken

18

German morale and will to fight. Arnold and his staff considered such attacks wasteful and not practical. They favored the precision dropping of bombs, during daylight hours, on specific industrial or military targets. When, at the Casablanca conference, pressure was brought by Prime Minister Winston Churchill to have the American Eighth Air Force join the RAF in its "mass" night bombing raids, Arnold quickly summoned his top expert in heavy bombing to defend the US tactics. He called on Major General Ira C. Eaker, Commanding General of the Eighth Air Force.

Prime Minister Churchill, with his cigar and bulldog face, was accustomed to having his own way during the early years of World War II, and many an American officer retreated under his fierce stare and frown-wrinkled brow. Eaker, the husky Texan veteran flier, backed down for no man, regardless of his title, and at Casablanca the general presented the case for American heavy bomber precision attacks so well that even the always talkative Churchill was silent. Eaker didn't base his arguments on theory. He based them on actual experience. He had received his wings in October, 1918, at Kelly Field, Texas, and had been flying ever since. After assignments all over the globe during the years between wars, he was sent to England in 1941 to observe RAF tactics against the Luftwaffe and the German homeland. When he returned home after Pearl Harbor, he was selected to organize and command the VIII Bomber Command, the forerunner of the Eighth Air Force.

On February 20, 1942, Eaker and six other USAAF officers—Major Peter Beasley, Lieutenant Harris Hull, Lieutenant Colonel Frank A. Armstrong, Captain Fred Castle, Captain Beirne Lay, Jr., and Lieutenant William Cowart, Jr.—arrived in England to set up the first American bomber command. It was a difficult job, one that not only required patience but courage. Even during the early formative stages of the American bomber force, the British insisted that it was impossible to bomb Germany during the daylight hours and that it was impossible to hit precision targets from high altitude while under antiaircraft and enemy fighter attacks. Consequently Eaker wanted to start flying bomber missions with American aircraft and crews as soon as possible in order to prove to the British that the USAAF doctrine was valid. Lack of planes, untrained crews, and bad weather delayed the first mission of the VIII Bomber Command, however, until August 17, 1942. On that day six B-17s of the Ninety-Seventh Bombardment Group took off from their base at Polebrook late in the afternoon and headed for the English Channel in a feint to divert the Luftwaffe planes from a main force of B-17s that took off from Grafton-Underwood later. This force consisted of twelve Flying Fortresses, including Ira Eaker in his B-17, nicknamed *Yankee Doodle*. After spending an hour climbing to 23,-000 feet and getting into a tight defensive formation, the American bombers took a course for the marshaling yards at Rouen-Sotteville, where they dropped 36,900 pounds of bombs on the railroad rolling stock, track, and buildings with reasonable accuracy. By 1900 hours that evening all the B-17s had returned safely to England, and the first American daylight heavy bomber mission was history. It was also a success, so much so that the C-in-C of the RAF Bomber Command sent a message stating: "Yankee Doodle certainly went to town and can stick another well-deserved feather in his cap."

The congratulations and the initial success of this first mission were soon forgotten by the British, however, and by January, 1943, when the Casablanca conference was held, the RAF was once again harassing the USAAF for their continuing insistence on the daylight precision-bombing doctrine. Eaker, at Arnold's request, told the assembled members of the conference that there was no ques-

20

tion in his mind that daylight bombing, as done by the American heavy bombers, could accomplish tasks that the RAF night bombers could never do.

"The day bombers can hit small, important targets such as individual factories, which could not be found or even seen at night," he said. "In addition, the accuracy of the daylight bombing is five times greater than that of the best night bombing."

He had the statistics to prove it. He also had the statistics to prove that the daylight bombing was safer and more economical. Yet Eaker knew that the USAAF record prior to the Casablanca conference was vulnerable to critics for various reasons—and the British critics, while not able to dispute his claims about the economics, safety, and accuracy of the USAAF doctrine, had several disturbing questions:

"Why had there been so many abortive sorties?"

"Why didn't the American bombers fly more missions?"

"Why hadn't the American bombers bombed Germany?"

It was this latter question that was most disturbing, not only to Eaker but to many other Americans both at home and in England. Eaker was quick to voice his own opinion.

"We certainly are not avoiding German targets," he explained. "In fact, I believe that in the near future they should be given a high priority for day bombardment. I hope that the Combined Chiefs of Staff will enlarge the scope of our bombing operations to include targets in Germany."

Eaker stated that his bomber command would be prepared to carry the daylight bombing to the enemy homeland by February 1, 1943.

It was this declaration and this statement of policy that set the stage for the fierce aerial battles over Germany

21

during 1943–44, which reached their peak during Big Week!

The question in everyone's mind as the American bombers prepared for their initial mission to Germany was whether the planes could make such deep daylight attacks without prohibitive losses. The first test came on January 27, 1943, when the B-17s were sent to bomb the submarine yards at Vegesack, situated on the Weser less than fifty miles from the North Sea estuary. Sixty-four Flying Fortresses took off from five airfields in England shortly after dawn on January 27, flew north over the North Sea and at 1110 hours crossed into German territory for the first time. The weather over Vegesack was not suitable for visual precision, so the bombers went to the port of Wilhelmshaven, the secondary target. The bombs were dropped from an altitude of 25,000 feet through a thin layer of clouds, forcing the bombardiers to sight the target through holes in the cloud cover. The damage to the German dock installations was not great, but the surprise daylight attack confused the enemy defenders. They were accustomed to the RAF night raids, but this was the first time they had exprienced a raid by American bombers during the daylight hours. While the Luftwaffe managed to get between fifty and seventy-five fighters into the air to intercept the American aircraft on their way out of Germany, the enemy pilots didn't press home their attacks on the bombers, as the more experienced Luftwaffe pilots stationed in France normally did. Only one B-17 was lost but the Germans lost seven of their fighters.

There was jublilation at Thurleigh, Molesworth, Chelveston, Bassingbourn, and Shipdham, the English bases from which the B-17s had taken off for the first mission to Germany. Unfortunately this initial success led many officers and airmen to believe that the raids planned for deep into Germany during 1943 would not result in heavy losses, that the guns of the B-17s and the escorting P-38s

22

and P-47s could drive off the attacking Luftwaffe fighters. This was an error that led to near disaster before the end of 1943!

Eight days later the American heavy bombers set out for Germany again, the crews confident they could handle any type of attack the Germans attempted. The target was deeper on this day. It was the railroad yards at Hamm in the heavily defended Ruhr area. This time there were eighty-six bombers, twenty-two more than had been on the first raid into Germany, and the largest American bomber force yet mustered for a raid against the enemy. The weather was not good at takeoff time in England, but the weathermen predicted clearing over the target area by the time the bombing force arrived. The prediction was not correct. The B-17s ran into heavy clouds over Germany and when it became obvious that it was not possible to bomb Hamm the mission was abandoned. The Flying Fortress formations were forced to break up when they flew into the clouds, since it was too dangerous for the crews to fly close together while "blind." This was what the Luftwaffe pilots had been waiting for during the long day.

As one straggling formation of American bombers attempted to drop their bombs on Emden, the German single-engine and twin-engine fighters roared in for the kill. Before the startled USAAF crews understood what was happening, four B-17s were shot down. One FW-190 pressed home its head-on attack so vigorously that it collided with a Flying Fortress and both planes were lost. This sobering incident brought home to the American bomber crewmen that the Luftwaffe had no intention of allowing the B-17s to invade the skies over their homeland without a fight. Any thoughts they harbored that the huge modern Flying Fortresses frightened the German pilots faded quickly, replaced by an awareness that they were involved in a five-mile-high life-and-death struggle, a struggle that would ultimately decide whether the Allies lost or won in the fight with Hitler. Without air supremacy over the Continent, the Allied could not mount a cross-channel invasion, and without such an invasion by the ground forces there was no way to defeat the Nazis.

During the month of February the VIII Bomber Command lost twenty-two of its effective strength of eighty-four aircraft, a loss rate that was extremely serious. While Eaker was aware that the day bombers were still learning their trade, he also knew that pressures were building both in England and in the US for the VIII Bomber Command to share a larger part of the air war in the ETO. It was necessary to extend the operations of the command, both in scope and weight, and to do so Eaker knew that changes in technique were needed. The handicaps faced by the VIII Bomber Command during the early part of 1943 as it tried to destroy the third of the targets outlined in AWPD-42 were formidable. Eaker received few replacements for the crews and aircraft lost to the Germans or through accidents . . . and the crews he did receive were inadequately trained for the combat they faced. The worst problem he faced, however, was the weather. During January, 1943, ten missions out of a scheduled fourteen had to be cancelled because of bad weather while in February only five missions were carried out. Nor did he have a blind-bombing technique for his bombers as yet. This would not come until the fall of 1943 when the Pathfinders would be used so successfully. If the weather was too bad for operations at the English bases, the bombers stayed on the ground. If the weather was good enough for the heavy bombers to get off the ground and then it was learned that the weather over the target area was bad, the mission was either called back or the secondary target was attacked. Either way, the assigned target was undamaged.

Despite the "black month" of February, the VIII Bomber Command continued its attempt to hit targets in Germany, knowing that time was running out if the deadline of AWPD-42 was to be met and the Allied invasion launched on schedule. Four days after the start of the new month, disaster struck the American bombers again. The VIII Bomber Command issued another Field Order listing the railroad yards at Hamm, deep in the Ruhr, as the target. Eaker knew that during such a long penetration into Germany, the Luftwaffe radar units would have sufficient time to alert all the fighter aircraft enroute and in the target area. In order to try to confuse the Germans, the main force of bombers headed northeast over the North Sea as though going to Wilhelmshaven or Bremen. Halfway between England and the Netherlands, the B-17s banked sharply to the right and headed southeast towards Hamm. Once again the weather interfered with plans, blocking the route of the bombers and forcing the cancellation of the Hamm attack. Three of the main-force bomber groups returned to England but the fourth, consisting of fourteen Flying Fortresses, became separated from the others and kept going. Surprisingly, once the group flew through the towering clouds blocking their route over the Netherlands, the sky cleared. The lone group continued on to Hamm and dropped its bombs with exceptional accuracy in cloudless skies.

Until the bomb drop onto the rail yards, the single group had met only scattered and light opposition, but it still had the long route back out of Germany to traverse, and the Luftwaffe was waiting. Fifty enemy fighters, both single-engine and twin-engine types, attacked the B-17s, making passes so close that the American gunners could plainly see the faces of the German pilots. Four of the fourteen Flying Fortresses were shot down and only a miracle prevented the entire group from being lost. It was proof, if proof were required, that a small group of unescorted heavy bombers was no match for the fighter defenses of the Reich. Another valuable but expensive lesson was learned.

Other lessons were learned, too. The VIII Bomber Command discovered that the group flying the best formation was seldom attacked by the enemy fighters if another group on the mission had its planes scattered across the sky in a loose, undisciplined formation. The Luftwaffe pilots respected the concentrated gunfire that a tight formation could place in their paths during an attack. They knew that it was much safer to face the scattered fifty-caliber guns of the less-skilled bomber pilots. Consequently, as the summer of 1943 approached, the overall formation flying of the VIII Bomber Command pilots improved greatly as the Americans recognized the thought pattern of the German fliers opposing them. Fighter escort was a valuable asset, too. The fighter pilots and the bomber pilots soon worked out a technique that was very successful on the missions into France. The gunners aboard the B-17s and B-24s were given the responsibility of protecting the rear of the formations from enemy attacks while the fighter pilots, flying ahead of the bombers, assumed the responsibility of defending the formations from head-on attacks by the Luftwaffe. This procedure worked very well. In addition, it saved a lot of US fighters from being damaged or shot down by overeager bomber gunners since the gunners, knowing the planes criss-crossing the sky in front of their bombers were "friendlies," didn't worry about them. Their orders were to fire at any "unidentified" fighter plane that came close to the formation, so they concentrated entirely on the rear area of the formation. Prior to the development of this fighter-escort technique, if a US fighter came too close to a formation—"too close" being a very general term to a nervous gunner—it was fired upon—and sometimes hit!

With such fighter-escort tactics and with a strong force of US P-47s and a few P-38s to accompany them, the bombers flying missions into France had light losses on most raids. The statistics were entirely different, however, when the B-17s and B-24s made bombing runs into the Reich, a distance much too long for the fighter planes. On April 17, 1942, the largest group of heavy bombers yet launched on a mission by the VIII Bomber Command attacked the Focke-Wulf plant at Bremen. The 107 Flying Fortresses that dropped their bombs on the German aircraft plant were a record number, but there was another record set that day, too. A record loss! Sixteen of the B-17s were shot down and forty-six others were damaged! Back in England, after the mission was over, Eaker and his staff tried to analyze the reason or reasons for the tragic loss of men and aircraft. The fact that the weather was ideal over the target area probably made the Germans suspicious that an American bombing raid was imminent and they had alerted their fighters. It was also learned that a Luftwaffe reconnaissance plane had spotted the bomber formations while they were still over the North Sea headed for Bremen and undoubtedly the German pilot had radioed this information, including the heading, speed, altitude, and number of bombers, back to his base, and this gave the enemy time to organize and concentrate his fighter defenses.

At any rate, more than 150 enemy fighters intercepted the Flying Fortresses, making their initial attack in force as the heavy bombers flew straight and level on the bombing run, a time when they were most vulnerable. Several bombers were shot down during this attack and several more during the persistent attacks during the withdrawal of the formations from the Reich. It was a tragic day for the VIII Bomber Command.

Despite the heavy loss on the April 17, 1942, Bremen mission the VIII had no alternative—if the objectives of AWPD-42 were to be attained—but to keep trying to penetrate the German defenses. The discouraging truth was that the German fighter force was getting stronger every day instead of decreasing as had been expected once the American bombers began bombing the aircraft factories. Allied intelligence sources had estimated that there were 350 German fighters on the Western front and in Germany in January, 1943, but this number had increased to 600 by June. Much of this increased production was due to the reorganization of the Ministry of Armament and Munitions by Albert Speer after the former minister, Dr. Fritz Todt, was killed in an aircraft accident. Not only were there many more fighters to oppose the B-17s and B-24s of the VIII Bomber Command but their effectiveness was increased. The Me-109's firepower was revised to equal that of the P-47, which was the American fighter plane available for escort duty at the time, but the FW-190 was much more heavily armed and a real threat to the heavy bombers. This improved and heavier armament of the German fighters coupled with the ever-increasing skill of the Luftwaffe pilots became evident in the statistics. During 1942 approximately thirteen percent of the heavy bombers were hit by defending enemy fighters but by mid-1943 this percentage had risen to more than eighteen percent.

There were no long-range American fighter planes available at this time to escort the heavy bombers to the targets deep in Germany. The P-38s could fly greater distances than the P-47s but most of the Lightnings were withdrawn from England to aid in the invasion of North Africa. The P-47s began arriving in the United Kingdom in January, 1943, but this new aircraft was far from being ready for combat. Engine failure and radio troubles limited their effectiveness seriously. Even when these problems were minimized, the short range of the Thunderbolts didn't permit them to escort the heavy bombers into Germany where they were needed most. Consequently by June, 1943, a decision had to be made concerning the future of the American heavy daylight bombing doctrine. Could it be continued without prohibitive losses against targets deep in Germany despite the lack of fighter escort? Could the one-third of the AWPD-42 targets be destroyed as planned by the end of 1943 with the equipment and manpower available to the bomber units of the USAAF in England? Was the all-important time schedule of AWPD-42 being maintained so that the invasion of the Continent could be launched as planned in May of 1944?

Many American and British military experts believed that the answer was no to all the questions.

In Italy, however, a short, stocky major general named James Harold Doolittle, better known as the "Jimmy" Doolittle who had led the daring one-way mission to Tokyo less than fourteen months earlier, was destined to change that no to yes during Big Week.

3
THE CRISIS

During the latter six months of 1943 it was obvious to both USAAF and Luftwaffe leaders that the battle for air supremacy in the skies over Europe was approaching its peak. The Eighth Air Force had completed its experimental phase and, although it had neither sufficient aircraft or crews, was preparing for an all-out challenge to the German Air Force over the Reich itself. The most critical question that was asked at High Wycombe, headquarters of the Eighth Air Force, and in USAAF headquarters in Washington, D.C., was whether the American heavy bombers could bomb the factories and installations supporting the German Air Force, which were located deep in Germany proper, without long-range fighter escort.

At the same time, the German Air Force began shifting its main defense efforts more and more against the American daylight bombers rather than the night-raiding RAF aircraft. Despite the fact that the RAF forces were larger, the daylight missions by the USAAF planes were more precise, caused more damage, and were of greater consequence to the German war industry. The Twenty-Sixth Destroyer Wing of the Luftwaffe deployed its three squadrons from Italy and the Eastern Front to central Germany and another wing, the ZG 76, was formed. This new wing was composed of pilots from various night-fighter squadrons, fliers direct from training schools, reconnaissance pilots, and crews from the First Squadron of ZG 1, which had been fighting in the Bay of Biscay area. ZG 76 was initially assigned to south Germany and later went to the Czechoslovakian sector.

These German units not only had the Me-109s and FW-190s but were also equipped with the Me-110s, 210s and the Me-410. These aircraft were fitted with 21-centimeter rockets and 3-centimeter, 3.7-centimeter, and 5-centimeter cannons, with which they could attack the American heavy bomber formations without getting within range of the B-17 or B-24 fifty-caliber machine guns. Consequently, with the increased number of fighters, better aircraft, and new defensive tactics, the Luftwaffe in June, 1943, was ready for the challenge the USAAF was poised to make to the Reich.

Washington, Bushy Park, and High Wycombe made the plans, but in the final analysis it was the men in the bombers who determined the success or failure of the operation. Many of the pilots were facing the enemy for the first time. Many had fewer than 300 hours of flying time. Major General David N.W. Grant, the air surgeon in charge of the health of all the Army Air Forces explained the problems faced by these fliers very clearly:

One look into the pilot's cabin of a B-17 will convince you that its flight is actually an engineering operation demanding manual and mental skills which put the driving of an automobile in the kiddy-car class.

The compartment is lined—front, sides, ceiling, and part of the floor—with controls, switches, levers, dials, and gauges. I once counted around one hundred and thirty. The coordinated operations of all gadgets would be difficult in the swivel-chair comfort of your office. But cut the size of your office to a five-foot cube, engulf it in the roar of four thousand-horsepower engines, increase your height to around

31

four or five miles. Then get into a flying suit, gloves, and shoes, all heated by electricity, put on a helmet with earphones, cover your eyes with goggles and the rest of your face with an oxygen mask containing a microphone, strap on your parachute, and it might be well to add about sixteen pounds of body armor.

That will give you an idea of the normal conditions under which these men work out the higher mathematical relationships of engine revolutions, manifold and fuel pressure, aerodynamics, barometric pressure, altitude, wind drift, air speed, ground speed, position and direction.

You may have to face an occasional pain from ears, bends, or intestinal-gas expansion, a touch of dizziness, numbness from cold, or the subtle comatosity of anoxia. There will be interruptions to man machine guns against enemy attacks. Also, due allowances must be made for a stream of machine-gun bullets or the burst of ack-ack shells in your immediate vicinity.

As a final touch to this bizarre picture of intense concentration, add the fear of death.

That fear was always present—alongside the courage that kept the USAAF crews going when the odds seemed too great to overcome. A man who had been behind a soda counter a year earlier now found himself behind a fifty-caliber machine gun in the icy-cold airstream of a B-17 waist window. An automobile mechanic who was warned to be careful when he test drove a $500 car he had repaired in civilian life was now solely responsible in the air for a bomber that cost at least a quarter of a million dollars and the lives of nine other men. A kid who had been playing sandlot baseball only months before was curled up in the ball turret of a B-17 protecting the "soft" underbelly of the aircraft from the German fighters and praying everytime an enemy antiaircraft shell burst near the fragile glass ball that separated him from eternity.

These were the men upon whom the USAAF leaders depended as they lined up the German targets for the heavy bombers. And the target list was impressive—and frightening to the aircrews who knew what had happened to former formations that had tried to penetrate the Reich without long-range fighter escort. Wilhelmshaven, Bremen, Kiel, Hamburg, Hannover, Kassel, Warnemunde, Bonn, Gelsenkirchen, Recklinghausen, Schweinfurt, Frankfurt, Regensburg, Emden, Wiesbaden, Saarlautern, Vegesack, Marienburg, Munster, Duren . . . the list seemed endless. The pilots, navigators, bombardiers, and gunners couldn't even pronounce most of the names. But it wasn't the pronunciation that worried them. It was the Luftwaffe— and the fear of death.

The challenge began on June 11, 1943, when the Eighth Air Force dispatched 252 heavy bombers to attack Bremen and Wilhelmshaven. Finding Bremen covered by a thick layer of clouds, 168 of the heavy bombers attacked Wilhelmshaven and thirty flew on to Cuxhaven, a designated target of opportunity. No fighter support was provided for the bombers since the targets were far beyond the range of the P-47s. As usual, the Luftwaffe was lying in wait on the bomb run, and when the pilots and bombardiers were busy trying to get lined up on the target area and holding the aircraft straight and level for the drop of the high explosives, the enemy fighters attacked in full force. The lead plane had both engines on the left wing knocked out with the result that the plane was difficult to control and yawed badly. Since the entire formation dropped on the bombs released by the lead bombardier and didn't use bombsights, the accuracy of the entire formation depended on this one man. Unfortunately, the lead bombardier of the B-17s attacking Wilhelmshaven couldn't line up his bombs on the target because of the yawing of the damaged Flying Fortress and the results were poor. Only a few bombs of the more than 400 tons dropped did serious damage, and none hit the main target, a U-boat building yard. Eight of the Flying Fortresses were lost, a high price to pay for the minimum damage inflicted on the enemy. Eighty men were missing from the English barracks of the Eighth Air Force on the night of June 11, 1943, and some of those who returned would never forget this initial mission of the summer-fall-winter offensive of the USAAF against the Luftwaffe. One of the men who had the mission stamped forever on his memory was Raul Hagerty.

Hagerty, a B-17 airplane commander of a lead plane in the Eighth Air Force formation, was one of the pilots who tried desperately to keep his bomber straight and level on the bomb run over the German naval yards at Wilhelmshaven despite the persistent attacks of the Luftwaffe. Concentrating on the instruments, he didn't see the two Me-109s diving in from the left. He wasn't aware that his B-17, the Lucky Doll, had been selected as their target until his left waist gunner gave the warning. Hagerty had time for one quick glance out the left cockpit window before the enemy fighters dove into firing range. He felt the Flying Fortress vibrate as his gunners attempted to drive the Luftwaffe planes off with their fifty-caliber machine guns. The thirty tons of bomber that had been flying through the sky toward the target suddenly lurched crazily as the left wing made a long arc towards the ground, pulling the nose around with it. Within the time it took for three flickers of the oxygen indicator, the B-17 was diving toward the earth five miles below.

The cockpit was in a shambles. A twenty-millimeter shell from one of the Me-109s had killed the copilot instantly and wounded Hagerty who lay slumped over the control wheel as the huge bomber dove towards the ground. The two Luftwaffe fighter pilots circled the plane once and, convinced that the B-17 was doomed, headed south. Not until the altimeter needle was passing the twelve-thousand-foot mark as it unwound did Hagerty stir. It took several seconds for the wounded pilot to focus his eyes on the instrument panel, which was now a mass of twisted metal with only the altimeter working properly. By this time the bomber was down to five thousand feet in its vertical dive. Grabbing the control column, Hagerty braced his feet on the rudder bar and tried to pull the control wheel back, but it was impossible even though he had cut the power on the engines completely. The airstream pressures built up on the control surfaces resisted his efforts to move them. It was then that the deseprate Hagerty sent the warning to his crews that many American officers and men had heard as they flew over enemy territory in a bomber—and dreaded.

"Bail out! Jump!"

The last moments of a dying bomber were always moments of confusion, desperation, and prayer for the men still in the plane. Even after the order to bail out came over the intercom system, it was not a mere matter of walking to the nearest exit and jumping. A crew member had to make certain that his parachute harness was buckled properly, that his parachute pack was attached to that harness, that he had his hand on the metal grip that would open his parachute once he was dropping through space. After he had checked these items, he still had the long walk, crawl, or dive to the nearest exit. If a B-17 were diving vertically or spinning wildly, the centrifugal forces on a man were enough to make it a superhuman effort to lift a foot. When he managed to get started towards the nearest exit, he was often knocked down by a sudden lurch of the doomed plane and had to start all over again—if he wasn't knocked unconscious. Once he reached the exit, he had to fling himself out into space in such a manner that neither his head nor foot hit the tail section. If he did hit the stabilizer or elevators, in all probability he would be killed. And he had approximately two to four minutes to accomplish the above tasks before the plane hit the ground or exploded!

Hagerty's crew was no exception to the rule. In the cockpit, after he had given his crew orders to bail out, Hagerty quickly checked his copilot and after making certain that the man was dead, released his seat belt so that he could slide through the trap door to the nose section and leap from the doomed plane through the open nose hatch that the bombardier and navigator had used. Just as he started to take his earphones off, however, he heard the voice of the tail-gunner.

"My God, Captain. Don't leave me here to die. I can't get out. Please. . . ."

The voice trailed off into silence. Hagerty now faced a decision that was just as important as any decision faced by the USAAF leaders in Washington or England, but they at least had a staff to help them find the correct answer. They also had time to think. Hagerty had neither. His situation over Wilhelmshaven on June 11, 1943, was one of many desperate situations to be faced by American and German airmen during the air war that was climaxed by Big Week, situations that called for lightning decisions, great courage, and feeling for others. Even with these attributes, a man often died before he could successfully resolve the situation. Hagerty was within a few feet of safety, only seconds from leaping into space when he heard the tail-gunner's cry for help but his reaction to the cry was automatic. He grabbed the control wheel again and pulled it back towards his stomach with the strength of desperation. He also rolled in all the elevator trim possible. Inch by inch the nose of the B-17 lifted from the vertical towards the horizon and he managed to level the plane off at less than 500 feet above the ground. Hagerty brought the damaged Flying Fortress back to England

with the trapped tail-gunner still alive and landed successfully at a base in the midlands.

Hagerty won his personal battle with the Luftwaffe that
day but the eight pilots and crew members of the B-17s
that were lost did not. In the days to come, more and
more Americans took off from their temporary English
"homes" never to return. The official USAAF records for
June and July give ample evidence to this fact:

Mission #63	Target:	Bremen and Kiel	26 planes lost
Mission #67	Target:	Northwest Germany	18 planes lost
Mission #74	Target:	Northwest Germany	1 plane lost
Mission #76	Target:	Hamburg, Kiel	19 planes lost
Mission #77	Target:	Hamburg, Hannover	24 planes lost
Mission #78	Target:	Kassel, Oschersleben	22 planes lost
Mission #79	Target:	Kiel, Warnemunde	10 planes lost
Mission #80	Target:	Kassel	12 planes lost

The above-listed missions, all to targets in Germany,
took a high toll of human lives and aircraft. As a respite
from the heavy air fighting taking place on the raids to
targets in the Reich, periodic missions were flown to targets in France, where fighter escort was possible. Losses
on these shorter raids were not nearly so high, and it became more and more evident that the only way excessive
losses could be avoided on the longer missions was for the
heavy bomber formations to have long-range fighter
planes to protect them. In the summer of 1943 this was
not possible . . . so an alternative was sought.

The alternative was the YB-40, a B-17 specially equipped to carry extra armament, armor and ammunition instead of bombs. A power-operated turret with two extra .50 guns was installed in the roof aft of the radio compartment from where it was controlled. Twin .50 guns replaced the single guns in the waist windows and a "chin" turret under the nose of the Flying Fortress was added. It, too, carried twin machine guns. Extra armor plate was added to protect the gunners and the internal sections of the aircraft, and the normal ammunition load was increased by more than fifty percent. The initial use of the YB-40 to escort the heavy bombers was in May, 1943, on a mission to St. Nazaire in France, and on this short-range trip the modified Flying Fortress was successful in helping the P-47s keep the Luftwaffe fighters at bay. However, it was soon discovered that the YB-40, which weighed 63,500 pounds compared to the normal load of a regular Flying Fortress of approximately 55,000 pounds, was incapable of keeping up with the other Flying Fortresses in climb and at combat cruise. Consequently their value was dubious and by August, 1943, the YB-40 was recognized as a failure as an alternative to long-range fighter escort and the modified B-17s were reconverted to bombers or to gunnery trainers.

As the month of August, 1943, began, the one optimistic note for the American airmen was the introduction of the jettisonable belly tanks on the P-47s, the only fighters available in sufficient numbers to provide the heavy bombers any protection. The Thunderbolt had acquitted itself well ever since it had become operational in April, 1943, despite the inexperience of its pilots. The big, heavy fighter could outdive any of the German fighters and it didn't take the American fighter pilots long to discover that this was an excellent method of breaking off combat with an enemy fighter when they so desired. The P-47 was no match, however, for the Luftwaffe planes in rate of climb or maneuverability, especially at low and medium altitudes. The Thunderbolt's greatest drawback, as far as the bombers pilots were concerned, was its lack of range, which did not permit it to accompany the B-17 or B-24s deep into Germany when they bombed targets in the Reich.

For nearly ten months engineers and test pilots in the US had been attempting to develop a jettisonable fuel tank that could be fitted to the P-47. Development and production problems had delayed the tanks to a certain extent but more important was the disagreement between US and British "experts" over the feasibility of ever developing a long-range fighter plane. American air planners had originally thought that no daylight bombing program that included targets in Germany could be successful without long-range fighters to escort the bombers; but during the initial American bomber raids in late 1942 and early 1943, when losses to enemy fighters were light, some of the "experts" changed their minds. They decided that the Flying Fortresses and Liberators, liberally supplied with guns, could fight their own way to the target and back without need of escorting fighters. This optimism soon faded as the spring and early summer missions of the American heavy bombers resulted in prohibitive losses, and they reverted to the idea that a long-range fighter was a vital requirement to the success of deep daylight bombing. This decision came at approximately the same time that it became obvious to the American air planners that the YB-40 was a failure as an escort for the heavy bombers.

The only hope that was left for the remainder of 1943 was to increase the range of the P-47 to its maximum ... and the only feasible method of doing this was to equip the Thunderbolt with extra fuel tanks. On July 28, 1943, most of the P-47s that escorted the heavy bombers to Oschersleben had makeshift 205-gallon paper-fuel tanks attached to them. These tanks were not pressurized for use much above 20,000 feet, and they cuased so much drag that the P-47 was extremely vulnerable to attack by Luftwaffe fighters. The plan was to fill the tanks half-full, use this fuel to cross the English Channel and reach an altitude of 20,000 feet, and then jettison them. On the Oschersleben mission the new tanks permitted the P-47 pilots to fly thirty miles deeper into Germany to meet the bombers and escort them home, and this deeper penetration, though slight, caught the Luftwaffe off guard. The Thunderbolt pilots pounced on a gaggle of sixty German fighters—while the Luftwaffe pilots were busy concentrating on Flying Fortresses that had been forced to drop out of the formation because of damage—and shot down nine of the enemy fighters before the Germans were aware that they were under attack.

In August a new type jettisonable fuel tank was provided for the P-47s. This was a pressurized seventy-five-gallon tank that could be carried until it was completely empty or the Luftwaffe was encountered, and the use of these tanks increased the range of the P-47 to 340 miles. This was a big help—but not enough. The disastrous air battle of August 17, 1943, was proof of that fact!

On this date, the first anniversary of American heavy bomber operations in England, two of the most critical targets on the APWD-42 list were scheduled to be bombed: the ball-bearing plants at Schweinfurt and the Messerschmitt complex at Regensburg. For this mission, the Eighth Air Force mustered the largest force of heavy bombers it had ever dispatched at one time, a total of 376 Flying Fortresses. Not only was it the largest American heavy-bomber force but it was also assigned to go deeper into Germany than any other American heavy bomber force had ever ventured. As though that were not enough records for one day, the B-17s designated to bomb Regensburg targets were briefed to continue to North African bases and land instead of returning to England, the first shuttle mission ever scheduled by the Eighth Air Force. It was obvious that the Eighth Air Force was pulling out all the stops, that it was going all out to prove to Hitler that the Luftwaffe could not stop the American heavy bombers from attacking any target in Germany they desired. Unfortunately, despite its growth and experience, the Eighth Air Force was not yet ready for such an undertaking.

In mid-July, 1943, Schweinfurt was the most important industrial area for the manufacture of ball bearings in Germany. A city of approximately 65,000 population, bordering the Main River in northern Bavaria and less than one hundred miles from Frankfurt, it was an excellent target for the American heavy bombers. The Vereinigte Kugellager Fabrik (VKF) plant and the Kugelfischer AG (FAG) factory were both located in Schweinfurt proper and employed over 17,000 workers. Two smaller plants, Deutsche Star Kugelhalter and Fichtel and Sachs were in the suburbs. Altogether, forty-two percent of all the bearings manufactured in Germany were manufactured by these installations in Schweinfurt. If the American heavy bombers could severely reduce the number of bearings this Schweinfurt complex normally delivered to the military and civilian users of such bearings in Germany, it would be a near-paralyzing blow to the Reich. US intelligence reports indicated there was little or no backlog of bearings in Germany, that there was always a critical need for more and more bearings, and it was estimated that a serious disruption in delivery would exert an influence on the battlefield itself within three months.

August 17, 1943, was one of the best flying days as far as weather was concerned that the Eighth Air Force had experienced in two weeks. The B-17s of the Third Bombardment Wing (still officially known as the Third Bombardment Wing) were scheduled to take off from their English bases first, followed within ten minutes by the First Bombardment Division, which was going to Schweinfurt. Since the Third Bombardment Division aircraft had to land at the African bases before dusk, it was impossible to delay their takeoff time when a sudden squall closed down most of the First Bombardment Division bases and consequently the heavy bombers heading for Schweinfurt departed England three and one-half hours after those going to Regensburg. Eighteen squadrons of P-47s, a small percentage of which had the still-scarce belly tanks installed for longer range, accompanied the Regensburg aircraft as far into Germany as possible. The plan called for these fighter planes to return to base, refuel and take off again to escort the Schweinfurt bombers. The hope was that the P-47s on the initial mission would engage the Luftwaffe and make it impossible for a large force of enemy fighters to attack the relatively unprotected Schweinfurt formations. It was a fine idea but the Germans refused to cooperate.

Before the B-17s of the First and Third Bombardment Divisions had left their bases in England, the German monitoring service reported the unusual activity at the airfields to the one Air Division of the Luftwaffe at Deelen. Knowing that such activity was a prelude to a large-scale operation, the Luftwaffe commander ordered several fighter *Gruppen* on the North Sea coast to move to advance bases west of the Rheims so that they would be ready to intercept the American bombers if they flew toward targets in Germany. When the 146 bombers of the Third Bombardment Division crossed the Dutch coast at approximately 10:00 A.M. that morning, they were picked up immediately by FW-190s of II/JG 1; but the German fighters did not attack while the P-47s were with the Flying Fortresses. The Luftwaffe pilots waited until the Thunderbolts, near the German frontiers, had to turn back as their fuel supply became low. And then they roared in for the kill. The fierce battle went on for ninety minutes without letup. As soon as one Luftwaffe Gruppen withdrew, another took its place and the German pilots unleashed every trick and device they had in their repertoire. The single-engine fighters attacked from all directions, singly and in groups. Once in a while entire squadrons would make a pass at the heavy bomber formation in javelin-up formation, which made it nearly impossible for the bombers to take any evasive action while under attack. The twin-engine German fighters cruised around the formations, staying out of .50-gun range and firing rockets at the B-17s. Some of these rocket attacks were very accurate and caused a great deal of damage.

Four Flying Fortresses were downed by the German fighter planes on their first pass, plummeting into Eifel country. Three more of the heavy bombers crashed near Hunsruck a few minutes later. Before the Third Bombardment Division reached the target area at Regensburg, it had lost fourteen of its aircraft, leaving 132 to bomb the Messerschmitt complex. The Luftwaffe received its first surprise of the day when the B-17s continued flying south after dropping their high explosives instead of doing a 180-degree turn and heading back toward England. The surprise didn't last long, however. As soon as the Germans determined that the Third Bombardment Division aircraft were going to bases in North Africa, Luftlotte two was alerted and this fighter unit shot down ten more of the Flying Fortresses. Altogether, the Third Bombardment Division lost twenty-four planes that day.

Three and one-half hours later the 229 B-17s of the First Bombardment Division on course for Schweinfurt crossed the mouth of the Scheldt and once again the Luftwaffe pilots were waiting. This time the Germans did not even wait for the P-47s to turn back. More than 300 enemy fighters were involved in the attacks on the First Bombardment Division heavy bombers as they droned

43

towards the ball-bearing plants and the resulting carnage was tragic. Thirty-six of the Flying Fortresses were knocked out of the sky by the Luftwaffe. Adding the twenty-four lost by the Third Bombardment Division, a total of sixty Flying Fortresses failed to return to their bases and 600 men were lost. More than 100 of the remaining B-17s were damaged, some so badly that they would never fly again. The only satisfaction achieved by the Eighth Air Force on August 17, 1943, was the fact that despite the violent attacks on their formations, the bombardiers did a creditable job of hitting the targets. Every important building in the Messerschmitt complex at Regensburg was damaged by the high explosives dropped by the Third Bombardment Division planes, and a large number of completed single-engine German fighters parked in the area were destroyed. At Schweinfurt eighty of the bombs hit the two main bearing plants and more than 600 machines were destroyed. Production of the all-important bearings was cut by two-thirds!

The mission of August 17, 1943, was positive proof—or so it seemed to most observers—that the American bombers could not bomb German targets without prohibitive losses unless they were given complete fighter escort. Many other observers of the tragic air battle of August 17, 1943, were convinced that not even complete-mission fighter escort would assure the success of daylight bombing missions into Germany. They believed that the Luftwaffe was too strong over its own homeland and any attempt by the American heavy bombers to penetrate the skies over the Reich was foolhardy. France, Holland, Belgium . . . yes! Germany . . . no!

After the Schweinfurt disaster, the Eighth Air Force didn't risk its remaining aircraft and crews on missions into Germany for five weeks. It resumed the easier, safer assignment of bombing airdromes and factories in France, Belgium, and Holland, where the fighters could accompany the heavy bombers all the way to the target and back. Losses were very low, more evidence that escorting fighters were a necessity. During the five-week lull in the bombing of Germany by the Eighth Air Force, more B-17s and B-24s arrived in England, flown across the Atlantic Ocean by combat crews assigned to the Eighth Air Force. By the first part of October, 1943, it was decided by USAAF leaders that the Eighth Air Force had reached such a total strength that it might be able to overpower the Luftwaffe even though long-range friendly fighters were not available to accompany the heavy bombers. They had deduced that the reason the First and Third Bombardment Divisions had taken such a beating on August 17, 1943, when they bombed Schweinfurt and Regensburg was not caused so much by a lack of long-range fighter planes as it was by the number of bombers that had participated in the mission. Although a record number of 376 B-17s had been dispatched to the two targets, the force had been divided between the heavy bombers going to Schweinfurt and those going to Regensburg, and they had penetrated the Reich sky three and one-half hours apart. By October, 1943, USAAF leaders decided that if a large force of American heavy bombers flying together challenged the Luftwaffe, the enemy would lose the air battle. It was another rosy dream that ended in tragedy!

On October 8, 1943, the Eighth Air Force sent 399 planes to bomb targets at Bremen and Vegesack accompanied by a large force of P-47s that escorted the bombers to the limit of their fuel range. Flying tight formation, so that all their guns could concentrate on attacking enemy fighters and throw up a wall of defensive fire, the heavy bombers' crews soon had their opportunity to test the new theory of the USAAF leaders. The Luftwaffe was strong in the Bremen-Vegesack area and on October 8, 1943, they did as they had done every time an American force of heavy bombers had attempted to penetrate the skies over the area. They attacked in full force! Despite the concentrated gunfire from the heavy bombers, the German pilots pressed their attack with skill and persistence; and before the Eighth Air Force units reached their home bases that day, thirty of the heavy bombers were shot down and twenty-six others received major damage.

The top officers of the USAAF were not convinced by the Bremen-Vegesack mission losses that the heavy bombers, if there were enough of them in the bombing force, could not take care of themselves regardless of whether they had fighter escort. On October 9, 1943, the Eighth Air Force was sent out again to test the self-defense tactics. Targets at Gdynia, Danzig, Marienburg, and Anklam were bombed at a cost of twenty-eight heavy bombers. The next day the heavy bombers were dispatched to bomb the vital Ruhr traffic junction at Münster; and during the period that they were without friendly fighter escort, a large force of FW-190s, Me-110s, Me-109s, Ju-88s, and Me-210s closed on the Eighth Air Force formations. The enemy fighters concentrated on one group at a time and the One Hundredth Bombardment Group, afterwards known as the "Bloody Hundredth," took the brunt of the attack. All twelve of the group's B-17s were shot down. A total of thirty heavy bombers were lost on the Münster mission, and it became more and more obvious that the big aircraft, despite their abundance of guns, were no match for the Luftwaffe fighters. It took one more mission, a total disaster, to convince the USAAF leaders, however, that this new self-defense theory was not practical.

Once again it was an attempt to bomb the ball-bearing plants at Schweinfurt that revealed the weaknesses of the Eighth Air Force tactics. Disregarding the tragic losses that had been inflicted on the heavy-bomber formations that bombed Schweinfurt on August 17, 1943, and the heavy losses during the previous three missions to Germany earlier in October, the USAAF leaders sent 291 B-17s to Schweinfurt on the morning of October 14, 1943. A force of B-24 heavy bombers was supposed to go to the target by a more southerly route, but it was unable to assemble its formations that morning and didn't fly the mission. The 149 Flying Fortresses that did go were from the First Bombardment Division and 142 were from the Third Bombardment Division, the same two units that had flown the tragic August 17, 1943, raid to the same target. Each of these units was assigned a group of Thunderbolts to escort them into Germany to the maximum range of the fighter planes and join them on withdrawal at a point sixty miles inland. This left the B-17s flying over enemy territory for several hours without any fighter escort, a real test for the self-defense theory.

The Luftwaffe waited until the P-47s turned back toward England near Aachen and then attacked. Wave after wave of enemy fighters made pass after pass on the formations, and by the time the B-17s reached the target area, they had already lost twenty-eight bombers. . . . And the crews that survived still faced the long trip back out of Germany. Despite being mauled so badly, however, the bombing was very accurate, resulting in the most damaging raid made on Schweinfurt during World War II. Three hundred and ninety-five tons of high explosives and eighty-eight tons of incendiaries were dropped on the target area and seriously damaged the ball-bearing plants. But the cost was high. Too high. Sixty B-17s and crews were lost on the mission. Seventeen other Flying Fortresses received major damage and 121 more were damaged but reparable.

Within a space of six days the Eighth Air Force had lost 148 bombers and crews and, more importantly, had lost air superiority over Germany. The self-defense theory was a complete failure. The daylight bombing campaign by the American Eighth Air Force had reached a crisis, a crisis that had to be resolved if the heavy bombers were to accomplish the job that had been assigned to them: Achieve air superiority over the German Air Force in time for the scheduled Allied invasion of Europe in the spring of 1944!

4
THE NEW PLAN

As a result of the October, 1943, missions conducted by the Eighth Air Force and the resultant heavy losses, which definitely could not be maintained because of logistics and public opinion, both the target list and the organization of the unit were changed. With the date for the Allied invasion of Europe nearing, more emphasis had to be placed on targets that would weaken the German Air Force. Time, effort, and supplies spent on bombing submarine yards, electric power plants, transportation facilities—unless they had a direct bearing on the German aircraft industry—served no purpose as far as accomplishing the objective of air superiority over Germany. Arnold convinced the Joint Chiefs of Staff that his Eighth Air Force could not bomb all the targets listed in AWPD-42 and still hope to defeat the Luftwaffe by the spring of 1944, the scheduled date of the invasion. He argued that his heavy bombers should make an all-out effort to attack the German Air Force, both in the air and on the ground, and any manufacturing facilities that contributed to the German aircraft industry. Arnold also explained that he needed more bases from which to attack the German targets if his target plan was accepted. He suggested a new air force to be established in Italy.

The Fifteenth Air Force, which was formally established on November 1, 1943, with bases in the Foggia complex of Italy, was organized with the hope that it would split the Luftwaffe's defense efforts and aid in the reduction of the high losses being experienced by the Eighth Air Force. Since it was predicted that the weather in Italy would be much better during the winter for flying than it would be in England, Arnold envisioned the heavy bombers of the Fifteenth Air Force bombing targets deep in Germany when the aircraft of the Eighth Air Force were grounded. In addition there were important German targets that could be reached from Italy that were definitely out of the range of the Eighth Air Force heavy bombers. Only those USAAF officers and British air planners who opposed the division of the American planes and crews voiced their disapproval of the new unit. Some of these officers still believed that in numbers there was strength and if the Eighth Air Force were expanded to a large enough force, it could fly anywhere and bomb any target it desired. The results of the October, 1943, efforts based on this thinking did not impress them despite the prohibitive losses. Arnold, Eaker, and many other USAAF planners, however, were now convinced that a long-range fighter was a necessity, that even with the heavy bombers being escorted to and from the target area by such long-range fighters, they would still take heavy losses. Consequently, any dividing of the Luftwaffe defensive units would be helpful, and they were certain that when Hitler discovered that the Reich was being attacked from the south by Italian-based American heavy bombers, he would order German Air Force fighter units away from the Western front to protect the southern borders of Germany.

Along with the establishment of the new Fifteenth Air Force and the decision to concentrate on destroying the German Air Force in the air and on the ground (code: Pointblank) prior to the Allied invasion of Europe (code: Overlord), there was also a reorganization of USAAF commanders. Since the British had air units in Italy and

North Africa and Malta and the French and Italians, after Italy's surrender, had units operating in the Mediterranean, it became apparent to the Combined Chiefs of Staff that an officer of high rank and proven ability and an expert in diplomacy was needed to command all these units if they were to operate efficiently together. Ira Eaker, the tough-minded veteran commander of the Eighth Air Force, was selected to head the new organization of Allied forces, which was designated the Mediterranean Allied Air Forces. This move, of course, left an opening for a new commander of the Eighth Air Force to replace Eaker, and for this all-important assignment, Arnold approved "Jimmy" Doolittle, at the time commanding officer of the newly formed Fifteenth Air Force. Major General Nathan F. Twining replaced Doolittle with the Fifteenth Air Force. The US Strategic Air Forces in Europe, a command organized to coordinate the operations of both the Eighth and Fifteenth Air Forces, was established with headquarters in England; and Major General Carl Spaatz, an officer considered by Arnold to be his best combat commander and a close associate of Lieutenant General Dwight D. Eisenhower, who had been selected to lead Overlord, the Allied invasion of Europe, was chosen as its commanding officer. Spaatz immediately selected Major General Frederick L. Anderson as his deputy for operations. It was these officers—Spaatz, Anderson, Doolittle, Twining, and Eaker—who planned Big Week, the series of missions in February, 1944, that finally defeated the Luftwaffe.

Long before "Jimmy" Doolittle arrived at High Wycombe, the new headquarters in England for the Eighth Air Force, his reputation as a flier and a fighter preceded him. His motto of "calculated risk" had led the short, daredevil pilot through a series of adventures that made his life seem unbelievable to those who did not know him personally. Those acquainted with Doolittle knew full well that every risk he took was well analyzed first and the odds figured carefully. If he felt he had an even chance of success, Doolittle was more than ready to try. With this attitude he was the ideal man to command the Eighth Air Force as it prepared for its final challenge to the German Air Force.

Doolittle, born in Alameda, California, on December 14, 1896, had been educated in Nome, Alaska, the Los Angeles Junior College and had studied for one year at the University of California School of Mines. He was commissioned a second lieutenant in the US Signal Corps' Aviation Section on March 11, 1918, and began a flying career that encompassed nearly every phase of aviation. As an officer during those early years, Doolittle made many pioneering flights—and at the same time found the spare hours needed to complete the requirements for his BA degree from the University of California. Not satisfied with this degree, he entered Massachusetts Institute of Technology in 1923 for special engineering courses and graduated a year later with an MS degree. Twelve months later he was awarded a Doctor of Science degree in aeronautics, one of the first men in the nation to earn this degree. Yet it wasn't the diplomas hanging on the walls of his residence that brought fame to "Jimmy" Doolittle. It was his courage and skill in the air, characteristics that were to be of great value as he led the Eighth Air Force in its February showdown battle with the German Air Force.

Early in his career Doolittle was an instructor at Ream Field, a remote airstrip across the bay from San Diego, not far from the Mexican border. One day a student pilot took off beside Doolittle's plane and shortly after the student was airborne he banked his aircraft directly into the path of Doolittle's plane. Before the shocked Doolittle could maneuver clear, the propeller of his plane chewed the tail section off the student's aircraft and it crashed, killing the student. Doolittle landed immediately and without even going to the crash scene ordered another student into the air to take the place of the one who had just crashed. Many of the pilots who witnessed the scene on the field that day thought that Doolittle had no emotions, no sympathy for others; but they later learned that the death of a fellow pilot raised an inner torment in him that he had to fight at all times to control. It was just that he believed that in a war death was to be expected. More than a quarter-century later—when, as commander of the Eighth Air Force, he had to order the heavy-bomber crews to targets deep inside Germany—"Jimmy" Doolittle faced without flinching the torment of sending men to almost certain death.

To many, Doolittle was the "Peck's Bad Boy of the Air" during the period between World War I and World War II. Restless, always looking for a challenge, Doolittle was the first to fly across the United States in less than twenty-four hours, first to fly entirely by instruments (during a flight in which he took off, flew a set course and landed without ever seeing the ground), broke the world's land-plane speed record in 1932, flew the Andes with two broken legs, and was the first pilot to fly an outside loop successfully. In his spare time he used his degree in aeronautical engineering to develop new aircraft and techniques for building and flying new aircraft.

In 1926 the daredevil Doolittle agreed to demonstrate a new Curtiss pursuit plane for the Chilean government. Unfortunately, a few days after his arrival in South America, he fell from a platform onto a concrete pavement and broke the tibia bone in each leg. When the Chilean government insisted on the demonstration, Doolittle had a portion of each of the plaster casts on his legs cut away and metal clips, with which he operated the rudder pedals, fastened to the bottom of each cast. A buddy carried him down to the plane and put him in the cockpit. Later, Curtiss representatives admitted that they had never seen a more brilliant exhibition of flying; and the Chilean government, after watching Doolittle put the plane through its aerial paces, was convinced it was the best plane in the world. Doolittle, pleased that he could fly so well despite the casts on his legs, decided to fly across the Andes from Antofagasta, Chile, to La Paz, Bolivia, to demonstrate the plane in that country. He ignored the warnings of his friends that this flight, over some of the most dangerous terrain in the world, had been flown only once before. He attached crutches to the gun mount of the Curtiss pursuit plane, tucked an extra thirty-gallon tank of gasoline behind the cockpit seat, and took off. At an altitude of less than 20,000 feet, Doolittle snaked his way between peaks and across saddles between the peaks so low the belly of the plane nearly touched some of them, but six hours later, still in one piece and good spirits, he landed at La Paz. To show that it was skill and not luck, Doolittle flew back across the Andes after he had demonstrated the plane in Bolivia.

As World War II became imminent, he left his civilian position as manager of the Aviation Department of the Shell Oil Company, which he had accepted in 1930, and returned to active duty. At first he worked with large automobile manufacturers on plans for converting their plants to the production of aircraft. In 1941 he went to England as a member of a special commission to study and evaluate the air forces of other countries. On January 2, 1942, he went to Washington and planned the first air attack on the Japanese homeland, a mission to retaliate in a small way for Pearl Harbor. After much badgering of Arnold, Doolittle received permission to lead the B-25s from the aircraft carrier Hornet to bomb Tokyo, Kobe, Osaka, and Nagoya in April, 1942. After bailing out, landing in a rice paddy near Chuchow, China, and returning to Washington, he was presented the Medal of Honor by President Roosevelt at the White House for, as the citation, stated:

> For conspicious leadership above and beyond the call of duty, involving personal valor and intrepidity at an extreme hazard to life. With the apparent certainty of being forced to land in enemy territory or to perish at sea, Lt. Col. Doolittle personally led a squadron of Army bombers, manned by volunteer crews, in a highly destructive raid on the Japanese mainland.

Two days after the attack, Doolittle was jumped in rank to brigadier general and in July, 1942, he was first assigned to the Eighth Air Force. Later he became commanding general of the Twelfth Air Force in North Africa, the North African Strategic Air Forces, the Fifteenth Air Force, and then, to replace Eaker, commanding general of the Eighth Air Force in December, 1943.

It didn't take Doolittle long to discover that the formidable task facing him—the destruction of the German Air Force—was just as difficult to achieve as his bombing of Tokyo had been earlier. On December 27, 1943, Arnold sent the following message to Doolittle and his Eighth Air Force:

> a. Aircraft factories in this country are turning out large quantities of airplanes, engines and accessories.
> b. Our training establishments are operating twenty-four hours per day, seven days per week training crews.
> c. We are now furnishing fully all the aircraft and crews to take care of your attrition.
> d. It is a conceded fact that Overlord will not be possible unless the German Air Force is destroyed.

e. Therefore, my personal message to you—this is a MUST—is to destroy the enemy air force wherever you find them, in the air, on the ground and in the factories.

Doolittle was aware that to successfully accomplish the destruction of the German Air Force it would be necessary for his heavy bombers to maintain a sustained attack against targets in the Reich during the winter months. To do this he needed long-range fighters and a successful method of bombing accurately through the clouds that covered Germany most of the time during the winter. The long-range fighter problem was one that had no easy answer. The extension of the range of the P-47 by the use external fuel tanks helped but was not the solution. During the middle of October, a group of P-38s arrived in England to help the seven groups of P-47s already with the VIII Fighter Command; and since the range of this plane, with the addition of two seventy-five-gallon wing tanks, was a maximum of 520 miles, it appeared that perhaps the long-awaited base-to-target-to-base fighter escort had arrived.

The Luftwaffe pilots soon nicknamed the P-38 *Der Gabelschwanz Teufel* meaning the fork-tailed devil, and respected the new fighter and its armament. Design work had begun on the Lockheed plane in 1937 to meet official specifications for a high-altitude interceptor that had a maximum speed of at least 360 mph at 20,000 feet, an endurance at full throttle of one hour at 20,000 feet, and the ability to take off and land over a fifty-foot obstacle within 2,200 feet. H.L. Hibbard, head of the design staff, was convinced that the only possible way he could meet these requirements was to equip the new fighter with two engines—which he did. Two twelve-cylinder Allison engines, each of 1,710 cubic-inch capacity were selected for the plane. Also, a radical twin-boom configuration was chosen for the fuselage, the booms providing convenient mountings for the turbo-superchargers, the engines, radiator baths, and main landing-gear wheels. Late on the night of December 31, 1938, the prototype was taken from its hangar and trucked to March Field in California for its initial tests. Despite several accidents, the P-38 was successfully tested and went into production, but it wasn't until 1941 that the USAAF received its first Lightning for evaluation. The first truly operational P-38 was the P-38F of late 1942, which took part in the North African campaign with mixed success. The air combat in that area was mostly at altitudes below 15,000 feet and the Lightning, designed for high-altitude interception, was at a distinct disadvantage. It was much more successful as a fighter-bomber, wreaking havoc on Rommel's forces.

The Eighth Air Force, however, needed fighters that could escort their bombers to targets in Germany and successfully keep the Luftwaffe away from the formations. Despite the fact that the P-38s had not been very successful against the German fighters in North Africa, when fighting at lower altitudes, Arnold was convinced that the Lightning could provide the needed long-range escort the Eighth Air Force required. At first it appeared that his opinion about the P-38 was justified. The Fifty-Fifth Fighter Group, the P-38 unit that arrived in England in October, 1943, escorted the B-17s to Wilhelmshaven on November 3, 1943, and encountered their first combat in the ETO near the target area. The P-38 pilots destroyed three enemy planes while losing only one Lightning, and they accomplished this feat while adhering to their strict orders to stay with the bombers and protect the formations rather than chase after the Luftwaffe aircraft. However, on November 13, 1943, when they helped the P-47s escort the heavy bombers to Bremen, it was a different situation. Left alone after the Thunderbolts had reached their maximum range and turned back toward England, the forty-seven P-38s discovered they were surrounded by a German fighter force five times as great as their own. Seven of the P-38s were lost and sixteen of the Lightnings that made it back to England were damaged badly. One of the damaged P-38s had lost an engine and the fuselage had more than one hundred holes in it. While the Lightnings had definitely helped keep heavy-bomber losses to an acceptable level on missions to targets such as Bremen and Wilhelmshaven, there was now considerable doubt as to whether the P-38s were the answer to the long-range escort problem as had first been thought. The twin-engines restricted maneuverability to a certain extent, and the P-38 had a tendency to pitch nose down at high speed as the result of compressibility. They were definitely outclassed by the FW-190 and the Bf-109. In addition it was the easiest of Allied fighters to identify because of its twin-booms and as a result was a favorite target of the German fighter pilots.

Taking all these factors into consideration, USAAF leaders switched their hopes to a new plane, which until this time had been considered primarily an attack plane—the P-51 Mustang! It was a fortunate decision since the P-51 unquestionably developed into the finest of all American war planes. After the end of World War II Arnold admitted that it was his own fault that the Mustang had not been used operationally much sooner than it was, but at least he realized his error in time to have the P-51 available for Big Week. Hitler, on the other hand, refused to listen to *his* own experts at about the same time and put his new jet fighter in production in time for Big Week! These two decisions, made months prior to the violent air battles of February, 1944, were important factors in the outcome of World War II.

The P-51 actually owed its development to the British Air Purchasing Commission, which had requested a new fighter plane to replace the outmoded P-40 it had been using in North Africa. North American Aviation was consulted, and within six months flight testing was started on a prototype, which was designated the NA-73. At first the USAAF ignored the new fighter plane although the RAF was delighted with the production models it began receiving in 1941 and used for ground attack. The low-rated engine with which the Mustang was equipped at that time made it unsuitable for normal fighter activities. However, it didn't take Major Thomas Hitchcock, the US military attaché in London, long to recommend to Washington that the Mustang "had one of the best, if not the best, fighter airframe developed at that date." He suggested putting a Merlin 61 engine in the Mustang frame and this opinion was quickly endorsed by Eddie Rickenbacker and Air Marshal Sir Trafford Leigh-Mallory. Two P-51s were fitted with the engines in the US, the fuselage was strengthened so that it could stand the stress of the additional power available, and other minor changes were made. Arnold was delighted with the modification results and in November, 1942, ordered approximately 2,200 of the P-51s. Unfortunately for the Eighth Air Force, it was another year before the first group of Mustangs were available for combat.

In September, 1943, two months before the new P-51s became available for assignment to the various USAAF units in the ETO and Pacific theater of operations, Arnold decided that no Mustangs should be assigned to any theater except the ETO for the remainder of 1943. Unfortunately this directive did not exactly solve the problem for the Eighth Air Force, since all P-51 units sent to the ETO ended up with the tactical Ninth Air Force, which was given the mission of supporting the invasion. Major General William E. Kepner, commanding general of the VIII Fighter Command, overcame this problem by "borrowing" the P-51s to escort the heavy bombers, since it was still several months until the invasion was scheduled.

Only one P-51 group, the Three Hundred and Fifty-Fourth, actually arrived in the ETO prior to the end of 1943, and it flew its first escort mission for the heavy bombers on December 5, 1943. This was a short bombing run to Paris, which did not really test the new fighter. The Luftwaffe, in fact, seemed reluctant to engage in combat with the P-51 during the month of December, 1943, despite the fact that the Mustang pilots flew escort for B-17 formations that bombed Kiel, Bremen, and Ludwigshafen. Consequently, as the new year started, it was still not known whether the P-51 was the long-range fighter the USAAF had been searching for. Only time would tell.

The second problem facing Doolittle, if he hoped to maintain a sustained attack against targets in the Reich during the winter months prior to the scheduled invasion, was the development of a successful method of bombing accurately through the clouds. He did not want to substitute "blind" bombing for visual bombing, but he wanted to be able to maintain constant pressure on the Germans, even on those days when the target was completely obscured. Since the early days of 1942, when the American bombers first began operating from bases in England, USAAF leaders had become well aware that weather was an important factor. Weather over England and Western Europe was extremely difficult to predict during the winter months; and it was a waste of time, money, and lives to send the heavy-bomber formations all the way to an enemy target only for the bombardiers to discover that it was covered by clouds and they couldn't bomb visually. Patterning the initial efforts after the RAF, Arnold laid plans to organize a "pathfinder" unit that would have aircraft equipped with radar and crew men trained to lead the bomber formations as a seeing-eye dog leads a blind person to his destination. The decision to organize the pathfinder units was much easier made than the actual development of such crews and equipment.

Initially the Eighth Air Force units attempted to use two navigational devices known as Gee and Oboe, both of which depended on beams transmitted from ground stations. The British had developed both devices and were using them extensively for their night bombers. However, both devices had drawbacks as far as the Americans were concerned. Gee was not accurate enough for use by the B-17s and B-24s of the Eighth Air Force. It was all right for area bombing such as the British did at night, but for pinpoint bombing during daylight hours it was unsatisfactory. Oboe, on the other hand, was excellent for short-range precision bombing but not for long-range missions such as Doolittle had to assign to his heavy bombers during the winter of 1943–44. In addition the British had a very limited supply of Oboe equipment, not enough to satisfy the demands of the USAAF.

Arnold decided that he would concentrate on a third British development known as H2S, which was a self-contained radar device that transmitted a beam from the aircraft that scanned the terrain the plane was flying over and displayed a maplike picture of the terrain on a cathode-ray tube indicator in the plane. In March, 1943, the British reluctantly provided the Eighth Air Force with eight of the H2S units to be installed in American heavy bombers on a trial basis.

Recognizing that the British would never provide ample H2S sets for the Eighth Air Force planes if the equipment proved satisfactory for blind bombing over Germany, Arnold asked for help from American industrial sources. The Radiation Laboratory at Massachusetts Institute of Technology agreed to supply US equipment of the H2S type by September, 1943. The American-produced equipment was designated the H2X.

Twelve Flying Fortresses had H2X sets installed by mid-September, 1943, and the planes and crews were assigned to the base at Alconbury, England, for training in the use of the equipment. An additional number of American aircraft had the British-built H2S installed and they, too, were sent to Alconbury with their crews. The Four Hundred and Eighty-Second Pathfinder Group was established at that base and, after a feverish training program, was made operational at the end of October, 1943.

While it was acknowledged that the H2X crews needed more practice, it was decided to let them get this practice over Germany! On November 3, 1943, eleven of the pathfinders—nine of the H2X, three of the H2S—guided 539 American heavy bombers to the cloud-covered port area of Wilhelmshaven, a target chosen because the city was situated on the coast line near an estuary of the Weser River and could be easily identified on the radar scope in the pathfinder. The heavy bombers, entirely dependent on the directions issued by the pathfinder crew, dropped a record bomb load of more than 1,400 tons through the solid overcast.

When the results were analyzed after reconnaissance aircraft brought photographs of the target area back to England, it was discovered that the bombing had been accurate and that the aiming point had definitely been hit. The bomb pattern was not as concentrated as it would have been if the bombing had been visual, but there was enough of a concentration of hits within the target area to damage many of the shipbuilding facilities. A fringe benefit of bombing through the overcast by the use of H2S and H2X was the fact that the Luftwaffe fighters were hesitant to take off and climb through the thick layer of clouds in search of the bombers. Consequently the heavy bombers' losses were light. Only seven of the 539 B-17s and B-24s failed to return home.

Radar bombing enabled the Eighth Air Force to step up its bombing missions during the months of November and December, 1943. Nearly all the missions were made possible by the use of H2X or H2S and, occasionally,

Oboe. Only a few visual drops were possible during the bad weather of this period. In December the Eighth Air Force dropped more bombs than it had dropped in any previous month—a total of 13,142 tons—and for the first time outdid the RAF Bomber Command. At the same time the Eighth Air Force was rapidly growing in size until by the end of the year it had twenty-six groups on operational status.

The day before Christmas, 1943, more than 700 heavy bombers were dispatched to a target, far more than had ever been sent against the enemy previously. The P-51 was available but untested against the Luftwaffe to any extent. "Jimmy" Doolittle was ready. The Eighth Air Force was ready. Operation Argument, the series of precision attacks against the highest-priority objectives, most of which were located in central and southern Germany—a series that became known as Big Week—was about to begin!

5
THE LUFTWAFFE IS READY

The USAAF had its "Jimmy" Doolittle; the Luftwaffe had its Adolf Galland! These two airmen, one German, one American, each representing the most courageous, daring, and brilliant personalities in their respective air forces, were destined to guide their planes and crews against each other in the most violent air battles of World War II during Big Week in February, 1944. The Eighth Air Force, led by Doolittle, met the Luftwaffe fighters, led by Galland, in the skies over Germany with the success or the failure of the forthcoming Allied invasion at stake. Both knew it was a critical operation, that the decision might go either way. It was a dramatic duel between two geniuses of air combat.

Adolf Galland was born in Westerholt, Westphalia, into a distinguished family that had held government posts ever since 1742 when the first Galland had emigrated to Westerholt from France. The only government assignment that young Adolf Galland was interested in, however, was as a pilot for the German Air Force; but unfortunately the Germans had been prohibited from having any military units or equipment by terms of the armistice that had ended World War I.

Gradually the German military officers who had survived World War I and were determined that eventually their country would have a strong military force again circumvented the restrictions ordered by the Allies and began secretly training pilots. Officers such as Hermann Göring and Albert Kesselring had no intention of permitting Germany to be at the mercy of the victors indefinitely, so they and others devised ways to start a new air force. One of the first methods they used was to train young, would-be pilots in gliders. The Allied restrictions said nothing about gliding as a sport, so it wasn't long before Germany had thousands of expert glider pilots. After Hitler came to power in March, 1933, and Göring became the second most important man in the Third Reich, the new German Air Force took giant steps where it had only been crawling during the previous years.

Benito Mussolini, the dictator of Italy and a friend of Hitler's, agreed to train selected Luftwaffe crews with his well-established Regia Aeronautics if international complications could be avoided. Consequently, in July, 1933, a group of German pilots-to-be traveled secretly across the mountains to Italian airfields, were issued Italian Air Force uniforms, and were absorbed into the training program as "Italian" students. Among this group of Germans was the happy-go-lucky glider pilot named Adolf Galland.

During the summer months of 1933 Galland and his comrades learned and practiced all aspects of modern air combat and developed the *blitzkreig* tactics that would prove so successful during the early years of World War II. The nucleus of the powerful Luftwaffe was formed during this period, and within six months after the pilots returned to Germany they were officially named as officers in the new German Air Force, as Hitler disregarded the restrictions the Allies had placed on German military units after World War I. (Galland, however, nearly missed getting his commission. While on a training flight in Germany he crashed and one eye was seriously damaged. When it come time to take his physical examination he memorized the eye chart, passed the examination, and continued flying.)

In 1936 an event occurred that gave Galland and his comrades an excellent opportunity to test the theories of aerial combat that they had been practicing since their training days in Italy. Civil war broke out in Spain and Hitler quickly decided that this was the chance his new air force needed to gain experience. He ordered a Luftwaffe "volunteer" unit to Spain to aid the forces of General Francisco Franco (Bahamonde), a unit identified officially as "88" but popularly known as the Condor Legion. Galland, disguised as a tourist and wearing civilian clothes, boarded ship at Hamburg with 400 other Germans. When he reached Spain, he was immediately assigned to a fighter squadron near Vittoria on the northern front. It didn't take him long to discover that the Loyalist pilots who opposed him in Curtis, and Rata fighters were expert combat fliers, and as long as he was assigned to fly the slower, outmoded He-51, his chances of survival were not good. It was a savage baptism of fire for him but, like Doolittle, he was a master at the art of calculated risk. If his plane was no match for the enemy at dogfighting, he decided, then he would concentrate on strafing ground targets. It was a wise decision because it kept him alive until the newer and faster Messerschmitt Bf-109 arrived in Spain. With these fighters, Galland and his command created havoc among the enemy forces on the ground and in the air.

Galland's experience with the Condor Legion in Spain was very valuable to him, just as it was very valuable to the newly-formed Luftwaffe as a whole. Actually Spain was a testing ground for the Germans who wanted to learn the efficiency of their new aircraft and their new tactics. Galland, trying to keep his pilots in tight wingtip-to-wingtip formation while engaging enemy planes, soon discovered that this technique, used by most air forces in the world, was no good when used with fast aircraft such as the Bf-109. The German pilots were concentrating so much on staying in a tight formation and at the same time not colliding with their comrades that they had no time to watch for attacking enemy planes. Galland and his men developed a technique of flying in pairs in a loose formation with six of these pairs forming a Staffel of twelve aircraft.

Galland, in Spain, became an expert at saturation bombing, the technique of concentrating on a city and practically wiping it completely off the earth. It was a technique that was to become familiar during World War II: Coventry, Dresden, Hiroshima. On April 26, 1937, Galland led his He-51 fighters to the Basque town of Guernica. It was a Monday, the traditional trading day for the peasants, and the central square of the town was crowded. A few minutes after 4:00 P.M., while the town's church bells were still ringing a warning to the peasants in the square, Galland and his He-51 fighters of the Condor Legion swept over Guernica at 500 feet with their guns firing steadily. After several passes over the town square, he led his pilots away from the scene to make room for the high-flying He-111 bombers, which rained down tons of bombs on the town. The attacks lasted until nearly 8:00 P.M., and the Germans left behind more than 1,600 men, women, and children dead.

Guernica was the first European town to be completely destroyed by bombing from the air, but Galland was well aware that it would not be the last. It was a much more tragic mission in terms of victims than the later Doolittle mission over Tokyo, but it was indicative of the brilliant planning and new techniques that both Doolittle and Galland were always developing.

Galland was recalled to Germany after flying more than 300 combat missions in Spain; and because of his experience he was given a job in the German Air Ministry, working out directives for organizing and training pilots for ground-support operations. His sorties in the He-51, strafing and searching out ground targets in Spain because the plane was too slow and clumsy for air-to-air combat, were put to good use by Göring. It wasn't the type of assignment that he preferred but he had no choice; and by the time Germany went to war in September, 1939, Galland had several Luftwaffe units ready for ground-support missions any place in Europe. In fact Galland himself flew on the first day of World War II, taking off from the Reichenau airfield in Silesia shortly before dawn. From the opening day until the final day of World War II, Adolf Galland was a man who haunted the Allied pilots day and night. By the end of the brief campaign in France he had shot down seventeen Allied aircraft, including three British Hurricanes, while his Fliegerkorps VIII Geschwader was supposedly assigned to ground-support missions only!

After France, Hitler issued his infamous Operational Directive Number 16, which declared:

Since England, despite her militarily hopeless situation still shows no sign of willingness to come to terms, I have decided to prepare a landing operation against England, and, if necessary, to carry it out. The aim of this operation is to eliminate the English homeland as a base for carrying on the war against Germany and, if it should be necessary, to occupy it completely.

It was at this time that the Luftwaffe faced the situation that Doolittle's Eighth Air Force would face four years later during Big Week. No German land invasion of England could be successful unless the Luftwaffe first commanded the skies over the English Channel and the United Kingdom. A seaborne armada would never make it across the Channel unless the German Air Force maintained complete air superiority overhead. Göring saw no difficulty in the assignment. "The enemy is already morally defeated," he told his Luftwaffe commanders. "Our first objective will be the destruction of his fighter forces, in the air and on the ground, together with the destruction of his airfields. This objective will be attained within two or three days, and that will be decisive."

It was little wonder that when Big Week began in February, 1944, Adolf Galland knew exactly what Doolittle's Eighth Air Force would attempt to do! He and his Luftwaffe comrades had tried the same thing against the RAF in 1940! Even Hitler's Operational Directive Number 17, issued during the Battle of Britain, sounded much like the message Arnold would send to Doolittle four years later as the Eighth Air Force prepared to try to defeat the Luftwaffe over Germany and obtain air superiority over Western Europe:

The German Air Force must with all means in their power and as quickly as possible destroy the English air force. The attacks must in the first instance be directed against flying formations, their ground organizations, and their supply organizations, and in the second against the aircraft production industry and the industries engaged in the production of antiaircraft equipment.

Galland, leading a Jagdgeschwader of Bf-109 fighters did the best he could to defeat the RAF and clear the Channel of Allied shipping, but it was a difficult task. When it became obvious that Göring's famed Stukas—Ju-87s—were neither feared by the civilians in England, as had been the case in Poland and France, nor a match for the faster, more maneuverable RAF fighters, Galland was promoted to a Gruppe commander and told that it was now up to him and other Bf-109 commanders to destroy the RAF in the air so the German invasion across the Channel could proceed as planned. Galland's

Luftflotte Two unit was moved to the Pas de Calais area, and for the next month he was over England nearly every day, desperately trying to lure the RAF into combat. Galland and his comrades made a good courageous try, but the British pilots were just as courageous and skilled as they.

By the first of September, 1940, many of the English Hurricane and Spitfire squadrons were so depreciated that they really existed on paper only. The entire RAF Fighter Command was down to a critical low level of both planes operational and fliers to man them. However, England was saved by Hitler's impatience with Galland and the other fighter-pilot commanders. Angry because the British night bombers were making sorties against Berlin, Hitler decided to retaliate by sending every fighter plane and bomber of the Luftwaffe available to attack London. This decision to bomb London and not concentrate on the RAF fighters, as Galland and the other fighter-unit commanders had been doing the previous weeks, saved the RAF Fighter Command. It gave the British forces time to rebuild, to train new pilots, to establish once again an adequate defensive fighter force.

Galland, who had already shot down forty-five enemy planes, was quick to criticize the new directive. When other Luftwaffe commanders remained silent, afraid to voice their opinion, he did not hesitate to criticize the directive. In fact, during the Battle of Britain, when Göring had been changing tactics so often and confusing the pilots, Galland had incurred his displeasure quite often. Once when Göring heard that Galland had been especially critical of the methods used by the Luftwaffe during the Battle of Britain, he called the cocksure fighter pilot to his office and demanded to know just what Galland thought he needed to win the fight.

"A Gruppe of Spitfires!" Galland told him.

Even the usually voluble Göring was speechless at the

70

remark. When Galland protested the directive converting his fighters into fighter-bombers, with orders to bomb London, his complaints were dismissed without even a reply. Perhaps in an effort to quiet him, Göring awarded Galland the Oak Leaves to the Knights Cross, Germany's highest military award. In the end, however, Galland was proven correct. The attempt to win air superiority over England and launch an invasion of the United Kingdom was finally abandoned by Hitler. The Führer gave many excuses for not continuing the operation, but the answer was plain to military observers on both sides of the battle: The Luftwaffe had failed in its attempt to defeat the RAF and bomb Britain into submission.

Four years later the Luftwaffe would be trying to prevent Doolittle's Eighth Air Force from doing the same thing to Germany!

Not only did Galland participate in the aerial battles of the period but he also was involved in the political and military intrigue that was a part of the Third Reich. It was Galland whom Göring called early on the evening of May 10, 1941, to stop Rudolf Hess, the deputy Führer of the Third Reich, who decided to fly an Me-110 to England to try to settle the war personally. It was just before dark and Galland didn't have a chance of stopping Hess, who eventually bailed out over Scotland and unsuccessfully tried to bring about a negotiated peace. Later in 1941—in November—Galland was shocked to hear an announcement on the radio involving a friend of his:

The Generalluftzeugmeister of the Luftwaffe, Generaloberst Ernst Udet had a fatal crash this morning while testing a new-type plane. The Führer has ordered a state funeral.

Galland, well aware of the dangerous intrigue constantly present among the top echelon of the Third Reich, was instantly suspicious about the cause of Udet's death. Udet was very popular with all the younger fighter pilots, a man who had an outstanding record as a fighter pilot in World War I and who was still one of the most skilled fliers in Germany. He was also an outspoken critic of the policies of the Luftwaffe, telling Galland on their last visit, "Fighters, fighters, fighters, that's what we need. Thousands of them." Yet Hitler was vehemently opposed to specializing in defensive tactics and building the fighters that such tactics would require. He wanted to be on the offensive constantly; and although the fighter production for the Luftwaffe was maintained at a high level, many of these fighters were used for ground-support and fighter-bomber missions during the same period that Germany began taking a beating from Allied bombers. Udet couldn't stand the pressures. He shot himself . . . and Hitler attempted to cover up the suicide with the plane-crash announcement.

Galland was one of the outstanding Luftwaffe aces who was the guard of honor at Udet's funeral. While engrossed in the services for the former World War I ace, two incidents occurred in other parts of Europe that would completely change his future. General Wilberg, a Luftwaffe officer who was held in high regard by Göring, was trying to get to Udet's funeral from Dresden when his Messerschmitt Taifun crashed and he was killed.

Even more tragic for Germany was the death the same day of Galland's close friend and the Luftwaffe's ace of aces, Werner Molders. He had been flying to Udet's funeral in Berlin from the Crimea, cruising through heavy clouds and rain, when one engine on his He-111 failed and he agreed with the pilot of the converted bomber that they would have to land at Breslau. As the aircraft let down through the overcast, it struck the wires of a cable railway, crashed, and burned. Molders was killed instantly.

Once again Galland attended a state funeral for a fallen friend, but after this funeral he did not return to his fighter command. Instead Göring summoned him to his side, and in a friendly manner, as though he had already forgotten the many arguments he and Galland had been involved in during previous operations, announced: "Now it is your turn. I name you herewith as Molders' successor to be General of the Fighter Arm."

It wasn't the happiest moment of Adolf Galland's life. He loved the life of a fighter pilot, was proud of the men in his squadron. The thought of sitting at a desk and sending others out to do the fighting depressed him. Göring, however, was firm. He stated that he had already discussed the matter with Hitler and that Galland was to go directly to his new office. Since Göring was making a personal trip to France, he informed Galland that he would explain the situation to Galland's squadron members and pass on his farewells to them. The only cheerful note about the entire change of command, as far as Galland was concerned, was the thought that now he might be able to shape the Luftwaffe more to his liking, that he might be able to convince Hitler and Göring to change some of the thinking about aerial warfare before it was too late.

It certainly wasn't easy for Galland to alter or completely change overall thinking about the use of the German fighter arm that had been standard operating procedure for several years. One aim that Galland hoped to achieve in his new position was the unification of command and organization of the day and night fighters. It was a long and difficult task but finally, in the fall of 1942, he achieved the unification that he had sought for so long. The fighter arm took command of both day and night fighters as well as all communication personnel involved in directing the fighter aircraft of the Luftwaffe as they defended German-held territory from the bombing attacks of the ever-increasing numbers of Allied bombers.

He installed double crews in the large radar control centers so that the centers had twenty-four-hour coverage.

By the end of 1943, while the Eighth Air Force was making its final preparations for Big Week, Galland had five complete fighter divisions including the control centers to direct their flight activities: Berlin-Central Germany Number 1; German Bight Number 2; Holland-Ruhr Number 3; South Germany Number 7; and the Eastern Marches Number 8. This was the all-inclusive defensive curtain that Doolittle's heavy bombers had to penetrate.

In addition to unifying the command and control of the day and night fighters, Galland also developed tactics for his fighter units to use against the ever-increasing number of B-17s that appeared over Europe in 1943. He was quick to recognize that his pilots were not prepared for the confrontation with these "flying monsters." They had been accustomed to attacking one British or American bomber; when an entire formation of B-17s approached them they were confused—and apprehensive. Galland figured out that one formation of twenty-seven Flying Fortresses could bring to bear at least 200 machine guns firing toward the stern, an approach direction the Luftwaffe fighters favored. He also discovered that it took twenty-two to twenty-four hits with a twenty-milimeter cannon to shoot down a B-17. With these facts in mind, he realized that the Luftwaffe fighter pilots would have to change their thinking and their tactics.

His first move was to brief his units to attack the heavy-bomber formations from the front instead of the rear. The closing speed between the bomber and the fighter would make it more difficult for the gunners aboard the big aircraft to hit the Luftwaffe planes, and fewer guns could be brought to bear on the attacking fighters. One of his elite fighter units, the Second Fighter Wing, commanded by Egon Meyer, tried this technique first; but despite several courageous passes at a formation of B-17s, little damage was inflicted on the heavy bombers.

Galland decided that the trouble was caused by the fact that the newer Me-109s had only one twenty-milimeter cannon compared with the older series, which had two such cannons. The new cannon was a better weapon. It fired faster and its trajectory was better, but it was not efficient enough against a B-17. He immediately asked for another cannon to be installed on all Me-109s, even though this meant that the weapons would have to be installed in the wings instead of being centrally mounted. His suggestion was ignored by the aircraft engineers, however, until the rumor of the trouble reached Hitler's ears. At a meeting, the Führer asked Galland which he considered best: one cannon centrally mounted or two cannons mounted in the wings?

"Better all three!"

Unfortunately Hitler decided to help the aircraft engineers with some ideas of his own, and one of the ideas was to add two twenty-milimeter cannons to the Me-109 in an under-the-wing gondola that seriously hampered the maneuverability of the plane. The modified three-cannon Me-109 was fairly effective against the B-17s, but when the P-51s began escorting the heavy bombers to the target, the gondolas had to be removed. Galland recognized that the FW-190 with its four cannons was much the better aircraft with which to combat the Flying Fortresses of Doolittle's Eighth Air Force. But there was a shortage of FW-190s and he could not obtain as many as he needed for the defense along the Western front.

As the Allied bomber attacks against German-held territory increased and more and more missions penetrated the Third Reich itself—some in daylight, although all deep penetrations were halted by the Eighth Air Force after the disastrous Schweinfurt raid of October 14, 1943—Galland tried desperately to convince Göring and Hitler that all defensive fighter planes should be based in an inner circle. If they were he could direct concentrated attacks on the heavy bombers instead of scattering the Luftwaffe fighters on an outer circle so that only a few of them could attack the formations at one time.

Hitler was furious at the suggestion. He did not want to permit the American or British bombers to attack German-held territory without a fight, which, of course, would have occurred if the Luftwaffe fighters had remained close to the Reich, as Galland suggested. The Führer didn't realize that by scattering the German fighter force, the Reich itself was going to suffer because the heavy bombers could not be stopped.

Not until the Hamburg inferno resulting from several large-scale raids by the RAF in July and August, 1943, did Göring finally become convinced that Galland's theory was correct. He called an emergency conference of his staff and commanders at the Wolf's Redoubt in East Prussia to settle the matter. Present at the meeting were Chief of the General Staff, Chief of Aircraft Production, the Air Force Commander, Central, the Air Communications commander and Galland. In addition many staff officers of the Luftwaffe attended. Göring gave a resumé of the Hamburg disaster and then stated: "The most important task of the Luftwaffe now is to protect the lives and property of the German people and preserve the potential of the war industry. To do this we must concentrate on air defense of the Third Reich."

This was exactly what Galland had been advocating for months. Everyone at the conference quickly agreed that the defense of Germany was of primary importance and that all efforts must be made to provide Galland with the fighters he needed, even at the expense of bomber production. All offensive operations by the Luftwaffe were to be canceled and the aircraft and crews scheduled for such actions were to be used, as best possible, for defensive purposes. It was one of the few times that Göring and his commanders all agreed on a decision.

"I will notify the Führer," Göring said at the end of the conference and there was not an officer in the room who didn't believe Hitler would see the necessity of such a decision.

They were wrong!

When Göring emerged from his meeting with the Führer a short time later, he walked through the conference room without looking to the right or left, without speaking to one of the officers in the room, and went directly to his private office. Later he called Galland into the office. Instead of agreeing with the unanimous decision made by Göring and his commanders, Hitler had become furious and screamed that a changeover from the offensive to the defensive by the Luftwaffe was "completely out of the question." Hitler had ordered Göring to resume the air offensive against England immediately, using every bomber and fighter, day and night aircraft, available! Galland could only shake his head in disgust. There was nothing he could do . . . not when the Führer had given the order personally.

It was a decision that had a decided effect on Big Week!

Galland, at approximately the same time, was involved in another controversy that, had his advice been accepted by Hitler, could have meant disaster for Doolittle and his Eighth Air Force. Early in 1942 he learned for the first time that designer Messerschmitt had under development a radically new type of aircraft, a jet fighter. Galland was fascinated by the possibilities of the new aircraft, and his statement at a conference pertaining to the development of the jet indicated his feelings:

We have now reached the point where the serious position of our fighter defense makes us call for an aircraft with at least equal performance to enable us to carry on; if possible, one with superior performance to outmatch them. We do not know what the enemy is doing in the whole field of aircraft construction but I consider that we shall be making the greatest mistake if we take too narrow a view in our planning and specify for a fast bomber without any account of the fact that the same aircraft, or similar aircraft, may in an emergency have to be used as a fast fighter rather than a fast bomber. I think that the technical department should specify for fighters as well.

Despite the fact that Galland's views, based on active service, were given careful consideration, it was decided by Hitler that the new jet should be a bomber not a fighter. Once again, the Führer refused to admit that his military forces were on the defensive. In his mind there was only one way to victory and that was to be on the offensive at all times. This error in judgment gave the Eighth Air Force an unanticipated extension of the deadline it eventually would have to face regarding the German jet planes. It wasn't until too late that Hitler realized his mistake and agreed that Galland should have jet fighters to defend the Third Reich. Big Week was over before he made that decision.

On May 22, 1943, Galland drove to the small airfield at Lechfeld, near Augsburg to test-fly the new jet plane, the Me-162, for the first time. He was more impressed than ever with the possibilities of the radically new aircraft, realizing that if his fighter units were supplied with the Me-262s in sufficient quantities, the Flying Fortress formations could be knocked from the skies over Germany. He immediately sent a telegram giving his viewpoint to Luftwaffe headquarters:

THE AIRCRAFT 262 IS A VERY GREAT HIT. IT WILL GUARANTEE US AN UNBELIEVABLE ADVANTAGE IN OPERATIONS WHILE THE ENEMY ADHERES TO THE PISTON ENGINE. FOR AIRWORTHINESS IT MAKES THE BEST IMPRESSION. THE ENGINES ARE ABSOLUTELY CONVINCING, EXCEPT DURING TAKEOFF AND LANDING. THIS AIRCRAFT OPENS UP COMPLETELY NEW TACTICAL POSSIBILITIES.

Galland knew that it was the fastest fighter in the world, that with it he could stop the Allied bombers and outmaneuver the Allied fighters. He was so enthusiastic about the Me-262 after his initial test flight that he decided to try to change Hitler's mind. He not only sent a telegram describing his feelings but went to visit Göring personally to tell him how he felt about the new jet plane and its possibilities. For once he found Göring very receptive. The Reichsmarshal had never forgotten his own World War I days as a fighter pilot and quickly sided with Galland.

But for the second time Hitler balked. Knowing that his experts all agreed with Galland, that the Me-262 should be put into mass production immediately as a jet fighter, Hitler still could not bring himself to the point to give an order that would have meant that the Luftwaffe was on the defensive not the offensive.

Instead, he stalled. He ordered the engineers and designers to continue testing and modifying the prototypes of the new jet plane until all the bugs were eliminated. Even the famed designer Messerschmitt was unable to convince Hitler that some bugs were always present in a new plane and that these problems could be worked out in the field after the aircraft was in production. Hitler refused to take his advice and ordered more testing. Galland was depressed, knowing that such testing would take at least another six months and with the formations of heavy bomb-

79

ers getting larger and larger every mission and the missions increasing in frequency, he didn't have six months!

As a final desperate move to establish a jet-fighter force, Galland secretly formed commando units of experienced fighter pilots to test the Me-262 against the fast-flying Mosquito bombers of the RAF. With the help of Messerschmitt and others, he stationed one detachment at the Augsburg factory and another at Rechlin, a few miles from Berlin and in late 1943 challenged the speedy British plane, which the Luftwaffe had never previously been able to stop. The Me-262, with its 520-mph speed, soon knocked several of the Mosquitos out of the air, proving that the jet plane was by far the best and fastest fighter in either the Allied or German air forces. As Galland expressed it, "I would rather have one Me-262 than five Me-109s!"

He was not to get them. Hitler was adamant. He would not change his mind and permit the Me-262 to be mass produced as a fighter, despite the fact that the Allied bombers were creating more and more damage to German territory. Göring, afraid to oppose the Führer, meekly agreed. The animosity that existed over the jet-plane controversy was made obvious late in 1943 when Galland told Hitler that American P-51s had penetrated the borders of Germany. Göring was furious and accused Galland of spreading such "lies" as a means of impressing the Führer of the need for the Me-262.

Galland shrugged his shoulders and said, "I told him the facts, Herr Reichsmarshal. American fighters were shot down over Aachen. This has been verified by our own people."

Göring, living in his own fantasy, became more and more angry until he finally screamed: "I herewith give you an official order that they weren't there. Do you understand?"

Galland, with his long cigar still in his mouth, grinned. "Orders are orders."

Galland knew that not only had American fighters been as far as Aachen but that they would soon be flying deeper into Germany. He had lost the jet-plane controversy and was disappointed but certainly not beaten. Despite the heavy-bomber attacks, the German fighter strength had been growing steadily during the fall months of 1943—even though the new aircraft were conventional fighters. In midyear there had been approximately 600 single-engine fighters on the Western front; but by late October Galland could count on nearly 800 such aircraft to help him ward off the Eighth Air Force bombers. Through his unified command and control system, he could direct his units faster and better. He had a large number of experienced pilots. In addition, Galland had secretly set up a modified inner-circle defense, although such a defense had been opposed and forbidden by Hitler. By this tactic he was ready to concentrate a large force of fighters against certain enemy formations if such Allied formations ventured deep into Germany.

Last but certainly not least, Galland had his secret commando units equipped with the Me-262 jet fighter strategically placed to intercept any B-17 or B-24 penetrations of the Third Reich.

The Luftwaffe was ready!

6
NO MORE TIME

By February, 1944, the destruction of the Luftwaffe and German fighter-production facilities had become a matter of such urgency that Arnold ordered an all-out aerial assault on the Third Reich. He knew that there was no more time, that if the Allied invasion scheduled for the spring of 1944 were to be launched, the USAAF had to break the back of the Luftwaffe. Arnold gave the historic orders to Spaatz on February 8, 1943, stating that the all-out aerial assault should begin as soon as possible and be completed by March 1, 1944. He was well aware that if Doolittle's Eighth Air Force and Twining's Fifteenth Air Force had not beaten the Luftwaffe by that time, their own forces would be so decimated and demoralized all hope that the Allies would have air superiority over the Continent in time for Overlord would be gone.

The primary responsibility for launching the series of bombing missions of February, 1944, belonged to the United States Strategic Air Force commanded by Spaatz, since this organization had operational control over both the Eighth Air Force in England and the Fifteenth Air Force in Italy. Spaatz immediately designated his deputy for operations, Major General Frederick L. Anderson, to take charge of coordinating the all-out aerial assault. Anderson, tall, raw-boned, and lean, was a friendly but determined individual who recognized the vital importance of his assignment. He had entered the air force immediately after his graduation from West Point and through the years had developed into a heavy-bombardment specialist. In 1940 he had commanded the first bombardier instructor's school, the foundation for a gigantic training program that developed during World War II when bombardiers were badly needed to join the crews of the heavy-bomber groups in both Europe and the Pacific. Later Anderson went to Washington as Deputy Director of Bombardment and in 1941 was sent to England to study the combat tactics used by the RAF. He was on his way home, flying the southern route, when he heard the news of the Japanese attack on Pearl Harbor. By the time he reached Washington, Arnold had an opening on his staff and Anderson filled it.

His affable mood was sometimes misleading, as one of the toughest commanders of the Eighth Air Force found out one day in England. Curtis E. LeMay, who at the time commanded the Three Hundred Fifth Heavy Bombardment Group at Chelveston, had his group ready to fly a mission one morning when the tall, gangly Anderson appeared at the airfield.

"I'm going along," he announced quietly to LeMay.

LeMay was chagrined. It was a long mission, one that was certain to lure the Luftwaffe into the sky in large numbers. He tried to talk Anderson out of his decision to fly the mission but it was impossible.

"I'm going," the determined general said. "Get me some flight equipment."

This, too, was a problem since the B-17s were already starting engines. The group could not be late taking off or it would not reach rendevous altitude in time to join the other heavy-bomber groups going on the mission. An oxygen mask was quickly found, two sergeants strapped a parachute harness on Anderson and tightened the straps while a corporal got him a pair of fur-lined flying boots to keep his feet warm. As Anderson prepared to board the

B-17, however, it was discovered that he did not have a Mae West. Since the mission involved a long trip over the North Sea it was imperative that the general have a Mae West in case the Flying Fortress had to ditch because of combat damage or mechanical problems. With the lead B-17 already taxiing toward the runway for takeoff, there was no time to go to supply and get Anderson the needed Mae West. At that moment a ground crewman spotted a gunner who had just returned from a practice gunnery mission over the Channel. He rushed to the gunner, took the Mae West from him, hurried back to General Anderson, and put it on him.

The startled gunner, thinking he was losing his Mae West and not recognizing the general (who had his back turned toward him), rushed up to Anderson and hit him hard on the back.

"Hey, buddy, that Mae West cost eighteen dollars and I'm not about to pay for it. You make damn sure you turn it into supply when you get back. You hear?"

LeMay started toward the gunner to reprimand him, but Anderson winked and held up his hand. Turning just far enough to see the gunner's face, he said, "Okay, I'll do that. Don't worry about it."

He climbed into the B-17.

As LeMay said later: "That Fred Anderson can handle any situation!"

The situation that faced Anderson in February was the most critical he had yet faced during the war. He was an advocate of the strategic principles outlined by a Chinese philosopher-general named Sun Tzu who had lived in 600 BC and quoted his maxims often:

"There are commands of the sovereign which must not be obeyed."
"Cut off the head of the leading concubine and the rest will behave."

84

The first maxim quoted by Anderson was his way of referring to the criticism leveled against the American heavy-bomber tactics of precision daylight bombing by the British. Anderson was certain that in the long run the USAAF policy would pay greater dividends than the area-bombing policy of the RAF. He saw the all-out aerial assault as an opportunity to prove the theory. As far as the second maxim quoted by Anderson, none of his staff had the nerve to ask him about the concubine reference. They were certain of one fact, however: One of Sun Tzu's most famous maxims—"The general who is skilled in defense hides in the most secret recesses of the earth"—wasn't suitable for Anderson. He had no intention of hiding anyplace. He intended to launch the greatest aerial assault of World War II just as soon as the weather cleared.

In Anderson's interpretation of the all-out aerial assault against the Third Reich, the objective of Doolittle's and Twining's planes and crews, was keep attacking, attacking, attacking, until the German aircraft plants, particularly those producing the single-engine Me-109s and Fw-190s, were destroyed or the Eighth and Fifteenth Air Forces were consumed. There was no alternative. The Germans were changing the sites of their aircraft plants, moving many of them further into Germany, putting some underground, and concentrating on a new type of industrial development, which they called complexes. At Leipzig the Germans had built their largest and most modern complex, which included at the center the mammoth Erla Machinenwerke, a final assembly plant for a third of all the Me-109s built in Germany and a fifth of all types of single-engine fighters produced. Component parts were shipped to Erla Machinenwerke from a large number of other plants in Leipzig and from Heiterblick and Abtnaundorf. In this same complex were repair shops and assembly lines for the Ju-88s and Ju-52. Anderson knew that this was one of the prime targets for his planned aerial assault.

Another important complex was located at Wiener Neustadt where Messerschmitt had the parent plant and at Regensburg, a city that had already cost the Eighth Air Force dearly, where the remainder of the Me-109s were produced. After the Eighth Air Force began bombing Germany, Hitler had ordered two more industrial complexes built. One was called the central Germany complex and included aircraft production facilities at Oschersleben, Warnemunde, Kassel, Anklam, and Marienburg; the second was called the eastern Germany complex and consisted of facilities at Tutow, Poznan, Gdynia, Sorau, Cottbus and Krzesinki. These five complexes—Leipzig, Wiener Neustadt, Regensburg, central Germany and eastern Germany—presented Anderson, Doolittle, and Twining enough targets to keep their crews busy for several months under normal operational procedures; but with a deadline of March 1, 1944, the task seemed herculean.

Doolittle, the master of the calculated risk, just shook his head as he studied the statistics and maps pertaining to the five industrial complexes his Eighth Air Force was expected to destroy in a matter of less than three weeks. He was never one to feel discouraged, but the assignment nearly overwhelmed him at the moment. Yet Anderson, who was briefing him on the plans for the all-out aerial assault, still hadn't finished.

"There are a few other targets we are charged with hitting also," he said dryly, unrolling more maps and charts.

Doolittle was especially concerned with the destruction of all production facilities that were involved with the building of the Me-109 and the Fw-190, since these two single-engine fighters were the enemy aircraft that gave his bombers the most trouble. Anderson, however, showed him a second list of targets that had nothing to do with single-engine fighters. The USAAF bombers were also expected to help out the British by striking at the sources of the twin-engine night fighters that constantly harassed the RAF bombers—the Ju-88s, Ju-188s, Me-110s, Me-210s and Me-410s. There were six complexes building these twin-engine fighters—Brunswick, Gotha, Augsburg, Bernburg, Munich, and Budapest. Only Budapest wasn't in Germany. To add to this list, there were also eighteen factories in fourteen different cities that built engines for the twin-engine fighters!

Anderson was also well aware, as was Doolittle, that the production flow could be shifted from plant to plant inside any of the complexes or to plants in other complexes. A complex was a big octopus and it was necessary to kill all of it to make it die. The affable Anderson, who seemed so easy-going on the surface, was prepared to sacrifice two-thirds of the USAAF heavy-bomber force based in England and Italy to "kill the octopus." This would mean more dead, wounded, and captured than were lost at Tarawa. As Arnold said on the eve of the all-out aerial assault that became known as Big Week: "We can expect heavier than normal losses since we are taking more than ordinary risks."

While Anderson coordinated the preparations for the assault between USSTAF headquarters and the Eighth and Fifteenth Air Forces, it was the commanders in the field who shouldered the responsibility of converting the words on paper into deeds in the air. As Doolittle remarked in mid-February as he waited for the series of missions to begin: "Man proposes but it is God who disposes." He was referring to one factor that was extremely important to the planned operation but over which man had no control—weather! It was a necessity that the bomber crews have clear skies over the target areas if the bomb drops were to be as accurate as expected. The missions were going to be long, were going to penetrate deep into Germany, and consequently were going to be very costly in planes and crews. If this cost were going to be high, the results had to be excellent to justify it. Yet with the targets scattered as they were, it was extremely difficult to forecast clear skies over all of them on one given day. Not only would there have to be a stable high-pressure system over Europe to guarantee such weather —as well as it could ever be guaranteed—but because the days were so short, there could be no fog over the English airfields at dawn or dusk. In order to reach some of the targets deep in Germany, the bombers would be taking off before daylight and landing after dark. Fog would only increase the cost through accidents as the B-17s tried to take off or land blind.

Arnold reached into the meteorlogical department of Cal Tech to recruit a young man with a radical and complicated theory about weather forecasting and sent him to England. The man was Irving P. Krick, who, as a sideline to his teaching job at the university, operated a weather-forecasting service for citrus growers, movie studios, trucking companies, coal merchants, department stores, and several other clients. Commissioned a major, Krick was flown to England to test his new theory against the unpredictable European weather. At the time of Krick's arrival in the United Kingdom, the Eighth Air Force was still almost completely dependent on British weather services for the forecasts. British weather maps and instruments, procured through reverse lend-lease, were a great help to the Eighth Air Force commanders but at the same time often caused confusion and delay because of unfamiliarity with some of the equipment and the problems of supply. Even British communication stations were used to send the synoptic weather reports since the USAAF had not yet set up an American meteorological teletype system in the United Kingdom.

Krick, however, ignored these obstacles and concentrated entirely on his new forecasting theory. Very briefly, his complicated system was based on his assumption that weather situations tended to repeat themselves and the sequence of phenomena that produced a certain kind of weather in the past would, if repeated, produce the same weather the next time it appeared. His procedure was to analyze the current meteorological pattern and then research past records until he located the same pattern. His forecast would then be based on the type of weather that had occurred when this pattern appeared the previous time. It was a controversial theory that many meteorologists opposed as inaccurate and unreliable; but since Arnold was dissatisfied with the weather forecasts the Eighth Air Force had been receiving through 1943, he was ready to rely on Krick for the all-important forecast that would launch the series of February, 1944, missions against the German aircraft industry.

The new theory, however, could only forecast weather conditions. It couldn't change weather conditions, and the wait for suitable visibility and cloud coverage over the target areas in Germany was a long and agonizing one to Doolittle and Anderson. When day after day passed and Krick could not predict at least three days of clear skies over the Continent—Anderson wanted a week if possible so the series of raids could be continuous—Doolittle pondered sending his bombers to the targets using pathfinders to designate the release point for the bomb loads. After all, the USAAF had spent a great deal of time and money developing the H2X radar-bombing system, so perhaps this was the time to use it and determine whether the system was a success or failure. Yet after studying the situation more closely, he realized that too much was at stake to rely on a radar-bombing system that had not been tested under the circumstances that would prevail during the all-out aerial assault on the German aircraft industry. The scheduled Allied invasion could not be risked on a relatively new and untried radar-bombing system. They would have to wait for good weather.

Meanwhile, Krick was studying European weather records that went back fifty years in a desperate effort to develop a forecast that would be accurate and suitable for the all-out aerial assault awaiting his signal. The only note of optimism about the delay for Doolittle was the fact that while he was waiting for the right type of weather his Eighth Air Force had grown to thirty groups and about 1,900 heavy bombers as Arnold sent all available new planes and crews from the States to the United Kingdom. Those that did not go to the Eighth Air Force were dispatched to increase the size of the new Fifteenth Air Force in Italy; and by mid-February, 1944, Twining had seventeen groups with approximately 900 bombers in his inventory. In addition, many more P-51s and P-38s had arrived in the theater of operations to escort the heavy bombers.

Doolittle's optimism was dampened somewhat by intelligence reports coming to his office. It was obvious that the Germans, expecting some type of massive aerial operation against them, were mobilizing their defenses. He had no way of knowing what Adolf Galland was thinking or planning, but he was well aware that numerous German radar stations were being installed along the aerial approaches to the Third Reich and that strong Luftwaffe fighter squadrons were concentrated along the same approach. Doolittle had no way of knowing about the secret commando units equipped with the new Me-262 jet fighter that were also lying in wait for the American heavy bombers. Nor did he know that Galland had reorganized the German fighter arm so that he now had a homogeneous force directed by controllers situated in underground centers. If Doolittle had known all these facts, his optimism would have faded much faster as he and the Eighth Air Force stood by for the word from Krick.

That word finally came on February 18, 1944, when Krick notified Anderson that a "good-looking pattern" seemed to be in the making.

"I predict that starting on the twentieth a high-pressure area will prevail over central and southern Germany," Krick said. "This should give a minimum of three days suitable for visual bombing and perhaps more."

It wasn't the guarantee of six or seven days that Anderson and Doolittle desired, but since time was getting short, if the March 1, 1944, deadline were to be met, they agreed that the operation should be launched. Spaatz was contacted and told about Krick's weather forecast, and on the afternoon of September 18, 1944, he gave the official word to make final preparations for the all-out aerial assault on the German aircraft industry.

The teletyped message went out to each of the heavy-bomber groups and fighter groups of the Eighth and Fifteenth Air Forces:

"Argument is laid on!" (Code word for all-out aerial assault on the German aircraft industry was Argument.)

For the next thirty-six hours Krick followed the forming weather pattern as closely as possible, and on the afternoon of February 19, 1944, he gave the final word:

"There will be three and possibly four days of good weather over most of Germany starting tomorrow!"

It wasn't an easy decision for either Krick or the men who had to order the operation to begin. There were two extensive pressure areas plotted, one centered in the Baltic region and one just west of Ireland. If both these pressure areas moved as anticipated, good weather was assured over Germany and the bases in England. The pressure system over the Baltic was expected to move southeast over Europe and drive away the heavy cloud cover in that area on the twentieth, leaving either perfectly clear skies or a few scattered clouds. If the system *didn't* move in the anticipated direction, the entire operation could be jeopardized.

Doolittle was worried. Very worried. It was one thing to sit in a comfortable office and order the heavy bomber crews into the sky on the morning of February 20, 1944, but his long piloting experience made him well aware of the other side of the decision—the hazards such an order placed on the bomber crews who were expected to follow it.

"What happens if we have a cloud cover five thousand or six thousand feet thick over the bases in the morning?" Doolittle muttered to a member of his staff as he looked at the cloud-covered sky late on the afternoon of February 19, 1944. He didn't want his listener to give him the answer. He *knew* the answer. Climbing at 500 feet per minute and at 140 mph, a Flying Fortress would require ten minutes or more to break into the clear above such an overcast and this was more than enough time to have ice form in the engines and coat the windshields.

"Of course, the pilots can use their de-icing fluid to keep the engines operating," he added, "and they can open their side windows for better visibility while they join the other planes in the formation."

His voice distinctively lacked enthusiasm for such procedures, however, and with reason. Doolittle had no desire to risk his crews to the weather. The moral responsibility of sending his men over Germany and into the lair of the Luftwaffe was great enough. He didn't want to send them to their death in ice-filled clouds.

While the weather over England was still bad on the afternoon and evening of February 19, 1944, another problem was encountered. When Anderson contacted the Fifteenth Air Force in Italy late that day to confirm the readiness of Twining's crews and planes for the next day's launching of the all-out aerial assault, he learned that there was a definite conflict in orders. Sir Charles Portal, chief of the British Air Staff and representative of the Combined Chiefs of Staff, stated that Prime Minister Winston Churchill wished all available aircraft to be used for the support of the ground forces fighting in the Anzio area on the twentieth! The Luftwaffe, after being relatively inactive around the Anzio beachhead for several days, was now attacking in force daily, and the British and American soldiers were taking heavy casualties. It was also known by Allied intelligence that the German ground forces were regrouping for a full-scale offensive at Anzio, and it was suspected that the heavy fighting that had started on the sixteenth might be the main assault. The Germans had nearly ten divisions in the battle against only five Allied divisions, and only air support could keep from breaking through the beachhead perimeter according to Portal. While the heavy bombers of the Fifteenth Air Force were supposedly based in Italy to bomb strategic targets in Germany, Portal had ordered them to be used on tactical missions to support the ground troops for several weeks. In fact, on the seventeenth more than one-third of the 813 Allied planes that had attacked German positions had been heavy bombers.

There was no question that the Allied ground troops needed the support of the Fifteenth Air Force, but so did Anderson if Argument were going to succeed and, ultimately, the invasion of Europe from the west. Anderson immediately notified Spaatz of the situation and Spaatz contacted Eaker, who, as commander of the MAAF, had to make the final decision on the use of the heavy bombers on February 20, 1944. He chose to help the ground troops at Anzio. It was a bitter disappointment for Anderson but when Doolittle heard about it he just shrugged. He knew that the burden of the all-out aerial assault was going to be the responsibility of the Eighth Air Force heavy bombers and their escorting fighters.

The uneasiness over the weather situation on the afternoon and evening of February 19, 1944, was acute at the fighter-group bases throughout England. A Flying Fortress had four engines and it was improbable that all four would ice up and become inoperable at one time. A P-51, however, had only one engine, and if it quit running, the pilot had only two choices: make an emergency landing or bail out. Neither of these courses of action would help the heavy bomber crews later when they were attacked by the German fighters over the Third Reich. A heavy, thick cloud cover over the fighter bases on the morning of the mission could be disastrous.

No one knew this better than Major General William "Bill" Kepner, commanding general of the Eighth Fighter Command. The 51-year-old veteran flier had seen a lot of weather, a lot of combat on the ground and in the air, and he was worried. P-51s were still not available in the quantities he wanted nor were experienced fighter pilots to fly them. He didn't want to lose a single plane or flier because of bad weather; and he knew what he was talking about through experience. By the time Kepner entered the air service in 1920 at the age of twenty-seven, he had seen more action than most men see during their entire lives. He served four years in the Marine Corps before World War I, transferred to the Indiana National Guard and later to the Twenty Eighth Infantry, where he served along the Mexican border. During World War I he led the Fourth Infantry's Third Battalion in the Meuse-Argonne offensive and later took part in the Aisne, Champagne, Marne, and St. Michel operations.

Instead of retiring after World War I, Kepner entered the air service, and with the same enthusiasm he had shown during his years with the ground forces he concentrated on learning to fly. He first became an outstanding balloonist and commanded several airship units during the years between the two wars. In 1931 he became a graduate pilot of conventional planes, and from that day forward Bill Kepner studied the techniques and tactics of fighter aircraft day and night. By September, 1943, when he took command of the Eighth Fighter Command, he knew exactly what was expected of him and his pilots and knew exactly how he intended to achieve the objective. He could handle anything under his control ... but he couldn't control the weather. On the evening of February 19, 1944, he periodically looked at the heavy cloud cover over England and shook his head.

"I don't like it."

Spaatz, Anderson, Doolittle, and Kepner, faced with the prospects that Krick's weather forecast might be inaccurate, tried to decide what to do. Field orders had to be transmitted to the various Eighth Air Force units in time for briefing, first-day targets had to be selected, the number of groups of heavy bombers to be dispatched to the selected targets had to be determined, as did the number of escorting fighters required for the bomber force. As the hours passed and the weather remained bad over England, it became obvious that a decision had to be made one way or another, regardless of the present conditions. Finally the pondering, the doubts, the confusion, the indecision were over. The USAAF had waited a long time, and with D-day less than four months away, there was no more waiting time available. The officers decided on a maximum effort for the next morning and within minutes the message was on the teletypes.

"Let 'em go!"

7
THE FIRST BLOW

When Gene Manson and the other members of the Ninety-Fifth Bombardment Group (H) reached the briefing room on the morning of February 20, 1944, they learned that they were a part of the largest American heavy-bomber force ever assembled. Sixteen combat wings of heavy bombers (numbering 1,028 aircraft), accompanied by 832 fighter planes, were scheduled for the first mission of the all-out aerial assault. In addition the RAF provided sixteen fighter squadrons of Spitfires and Mustangs to help protect the heavy bombers. It didn't take long for Manson and the other pilots studying the maps in briefing rooms across the midlands of England that morning to realize they would need all the help they could get.

The industrial complex at Leipzig and the eastern German complex, sometimes called the Tutow complex, were the main objectives of the heavy bombers on February 20, 1944. Altogether there were twelve targets, including units of the Gotha and Bernburg complex in central Germany. At Leipzig the Me-109 and Ju-88 plants were the targets; the Ju-88, Ju-188, and Ju-52 plants at Bernburg; the Me-110 plants at Brunswick and Gotha; the FW-190 plants at Tutow and Oschersleben; and the He-111 plant at Rostock. The planes of the First Bombardment Division, the heavy bombers with the eighty-inch white triangle painted on each side of the vertical fin as their identification symbol, and the Second Bombardment Division planes, which used the same size circle on the tail section as their symbol, feinted at Berlin after taking off from England. Short of the Third Reich capital, however, the two divisions abruptly changed course. The First Division planes struck at Leipzig, Oschersleben, and Bernburg while the Second Division heavy bombers bombed Magdeburg, Brunswick, and Gotha. The aircraft with the white squares on their vertical fins, the Third Bombardment Division, flew a wide arc over the North Sea, crossed Denmark, and bombed Tutow and Rostock.

As Manson discovered at the briefing for the Ninety Fifth Bombardment Group (H), the Third Division heavy bombers had no figher escort on their trip to the target and return since Doolittle knew that the B-17s and B-24s attacking central Germany would encounter the stiffest resistance from the Luftwaffe. He decided that it was an acceptable calculated risk to send the Third Division heavy bombers across the North Sea without any accompanying P-51s or P-38s, since their route lay largely beyond the lanes usually defended by the Luftwaffe. He also arranged to have the main force of heavy bombers, which was headed for central Germany, enter the enemy radar screen in time to stop large forces of enemy fighters from chasing the Third Division planes over the North Sea. Doolittle knew that Galland would be more interested in defending Berlin and the surrounding area than he would the northern target areas.

Fortunately Krick was correct about the weather. The bases in England were not fogged in early on the morning of the twentieth, as many had thought they would be after the heavy cloud cover of the night before. There was very little difficulty involved in the takeoff and assembly of the 1,028 heavy bombers high in the skies over their United Kingdom bases; and, in general, reconnaissance aircraft returning from dawn flights over the target areas predicted visual conditions for bombing.

Manson and the Ninety-Fifth Group, accompanied by the other Third Division planes, climbed slowly to altitude as they headed northeast over the North Sea; but the aircraft of the First and Second Division had to attain their bombing altitude prior to crossing the English Channel since the enemy had numerous antiaircraft guns along the coastline of the Continent, which made a low-altitude crossing too hazardous. The three American divisions of heavy bombers each assembled and left England on time, however, without incident.

Doolittle silently congratulated the Eighth Air Force on a good beginning of a tough operation. He hoped that the remainder of the mission would go as smoothly ... although he anticipated a full-scale effort by Galland's fighters to stop the bombers once they were spotted on the German radar screen.

"Achtung! Achtung!"

The early warnings from the German Freya apparatus on the English Channel Coast reached the three Luftwaffe fighter divisions assigned to the central Germany defense area within minutes after the first B-17 of the Four Hundred First Group, which was leading the First Division, penetrated the sky over the Continent. Colonel Hajo Herrmann, commanding officer of No. 1 Division, based at Dobertiz near Berlin, received the warning while he was still in his office and immediately alerted his pilots. After checking on the progress of the American bombers for a few minutes, he was certain that the Eighth Air Force intended to bomb Berlin.

"They will never reach the capital," he vowed as he hurried to the airfield.

Major General Max Ibel who commanded Number Two Division at Stade on the Elbe was not so certain. The veteran Luftwaffe officer had been fighting the RAF and the American airmen long enough to know that the situation was not always as it appeared.

"Perhaps they are going to Berlin," he muttered as he checked the plots as they were relayed to him, "but perhaps they are only pretending." He looked at the maps on the table beside him. The American bombers could very easily turn away from Berlin at the last moment and head for many choice targets in that area, he knew. His eyes centered on Leipzig ... and stayed there. Perhaps the Americans intended to bomb the aircraft factories at Leipzig! Ibel decided that he would wait for a while before he committed his Me-109s. If the B-17s turned towards Leipzig, as he suspected they might, he wanted to attack at that time.

Number Three Division at Deelen, Holland, was commanded by a veteran of the Battle of Britain, Colonel Walter Grabmann. He didn't have as much time as the other two German officers to commit his twin-engine fighters, so as soon as he was certain that the heavy-bomber stream was definitely on course for central Germany, he ordered his pilots into the air.

"Crews prepare for immediate takeoff!"

Galland, listening at central control center, smiled as he heard Grabmann's order. He was delighted with the efficiency of his united control system, the system he had installed after becoming General of the Fighter Arm. Through this system he could and would use his new defense principle of "mass against mass." Instead of scattering his fighter force throughout the skies of Europe, he could concentrate most of them into one devastating attacking force and launch that force against Doolittle's bomber formations at their most vulnerable point.

"The American heavy bombers will never reach Berlin today!"

As the Four Hundred First Group led the First and Second Division bombers towards the Leipzig complex, the Ninety-Fifth Group and the rest of the Third Division climbed steadily higher and higher as they crossed the North Sea towards Rostock and Tutow. Since they had no fighter escort, the crews of the Third Division silently prayed that the Luftwaffe would be so busy with the heavy bombers of the other two divisions they would not detect their formations so far to the north. They were aware that if the German fighters attacked in force, it would be an aerial massacre. During the first two hours, however, the heavy bombers droned across the water without incident, and with each passing minute Manson and the other crew members of the Third Division became more confident that Doolittle had been correct, that the Luftwaffe would not detect their formations on their radar screens until it was too late. Fortunately for their peace of mind they did not know about the desperate and unusual aerial battle being fought in their behalf a few miles further west.

Lieutenant Guy Reed of Homewood, Wisconsin, had left an air base in Scotland before dawn on the morning of February 20, 1944, in a Flying Fortress modified for reconnaissance and weather flights. His assignment was to verify Krick's forecast and to send back radio reports to Eighth Air Force headquarters on weather conditions over the North Atlantic and the North Sea, so that Anderson and Doolittle could recall the heavy bombers if it appeared that bad weather conditions were going to close the English bases by the time of return. As he banked his B-17 to the west over the North Sea and prepared to head out over the North Atlantic, his radio operator called him on the interphone.

"Pilot, this is Radio. I'm picking up a strange radio beam on the same frequency used by Prestwick."

Reed was on the alert immediately. He had been briefed to try and detect a ghost radio beam that had cost the lives of many American airmen. When a new group of replacement pilots for the Eighth Air Force flew the Atlantic Ocean on their way to the ETO, they homed in on a radio signal emanating from Prestwick, Scotland, which guided them to safety. But in recent months the Germans had been transmitting a signal on the same frequency, using the same identification. This signal led the bombers far to the north of their expected landfall, and when the B-17s exhausted their fuel supply, they had to ditch.

"Is the signal strong?" Reed asked.

"Very strong."

"Roger. We'll home in on it."

Within fifteen minutes the needle on his radio compass began to swing very fast, a sure sign that he was getting close to the source of the signal. The sky over the North Sea was cloudy and visibility was down to a quarter mile, so Reed was startled when the B-17 suddenly broke out of the clouds into a perfectly clear sky and he saw a German He-177 directly ahead of him. The tail-gunner of the big German reconnaissance plane saw the B-17 at the same instant and a moment later, after the Luftwaffe pilot was alerted, the He-177 banked sharply to the left.

"Is the signal coming from that He-177?" Reed asked the radio operator.

"Roger."

Reed was surprised and he knew that Doolittle and his staff would also be surprised to learn that the ghost radio signal was coming from a German plane instead of a submarine as had been expected. But he wasn't so surprised he didn't realize there was another danger involved in the situation: Would the He-177 crew spot the formations of the Third Division, which at that moment were climbing to altitude over the North Sea less than thirty miles further east? If the German crew saw the B-17 formations, Reed knew the pilot would immediately radio the information, including course and altitude, to the

Luftwaffe units further south, and the unescorted Flying Fortresses would be in serious danger. They were still far enough south to make a concentrated attack by the Luftwaffe a distinct possibility. Reed knew he had no alternative.

"Pilot to crew. We're going to attack."

In one of the most unusual air battles of World War II, Reed in his four-engine B-17 launched a fighter-type attack on the He-177. The German plane was also powered by four engines—two in each nacelle, geared together to drive one propeller. Its 120-foot wingspan was half again as large as that of the B-17, so it was really a battle of the giants. Doggedly Reed chased the He-177, which desperately tried to hide in the clouds, and once, in the hazy visibility, nearly collided with it. Pushing the nose down to avoid a midair collision, Reed grazed the tail section of the German plane, and as he leveled out beneath it his gunners raked the belly of the Heinkel. Tracers walked a line across the German plane's fuselage, tearing and ripping the outer skin of the aircraft. Reed banked to the right, walked the four throttles of the B-17 steadily forward until he had full power, and pulled the control wheel yoke back hard. The Flying Fortress climbed steeply until it was directly on the tail of the huge German plane.

"Let them have it!" Reed called over the interphone.

The B-17 vibrated as the gunners opened fire. The He-177 veered away, fell off on its left wing and started a steep dive toward the North Sea. The B-17 stayed right with the German plane, the gunners firing continually. The German pilot, however, was not beaten yet. At 3,000 feet, he pulled the nose of the He-177 up, cut the throttles back, and dropped full flaps and his landing gear. The big plane seemed to stop in midair. Taken by surprise, Reed overran the other plane; and, as the B-17 passed to the left of the He-177, the German gunners opened fire. One shell from the initial barrage killed the right waist gunner. Others knocked the dome off the top turret and jammed the rudder so that the Flying Fortress constantly wanted to turn to the left. For minutes that seemed an eternity, the two giants sat broadside to each other, like two battleships on the sea, firing point blank.

The He-177 gave way first. A fifty-caliber shell through the cockpit window convinced the German pilot that it was time to make a run for home. He banked sharply to the right, but at that moment he lost power on the right side as a stream of machine-gun fire hit the right nacelle. Before the German pilot could counteract the loss of power on the same side that he had banked so steeply, he lost control of the He-177 and it went into a spin. The crew didn't even have time to bail out before the doomed plane plunged into the North Sea.

The Third Division Flying Fortresses continued northeast completely unaware of Reed's action, a few miles to the west, which prevented the Luftwaffe from discovering their presence earlier than planned and disrupting the surprise element of the mission. Reed was able to fly his damaged B-17 back to Scotland, where he made a successful emergency landing.

Nearly two hundred miles southeast of the Third Division Flying Fortresses, Luftwaffe Major General Max Ibel was still waiting before ordering his Number Two Division Me-109s into the air. Ibel was a patient man, a German flier who had been fighting the British pilots for a long time; and now, as he pitted his experience against the American heavy-bomber formations, he refused to panic. He remembered the days of the Dunkirk battles, when his Geschwader JG 27 cleared the skies of British planes because of his coolness under pressure.

He had devised a plan for refueling and briefing so that each of his Me-109s could fly at least four or five sorties in one day. On May 12, 1940, using this operating procedure, Ibel's pilots had shot down twenty-eight British fighters and bombers over the Dunkirk area, at a cost of four of his own planes. That evening an urgent telegram arrived at RAF headquarters near Chauny-sur-Oise that indicated the seriousness of Ibel's success as far as the British were concerned. The telegram, from the Chief of the Air Staff in London, stated:

WE CANNOT CONTINUE INDEFINITELY AT THIS RATE. IF WE EXPEND ALL OUT EFFORTS IN THE EARLY STAGES OF THE BATTLE WE SHALL NOT BE ABLE TO OPERATE EFFECTIVELY WHEN THE REALLY CRITICAL PHASE COMES.

It was a prophetic prediction since the British finally had to abandon operations at Dunkirk.

The Eighth Air Force divisions heading towards Germany, however, had no intention of abandoning their mission, and Ibel was well aware of this fact. All he wanted to do was wait until he was certain the American heavy bombers were going to bomb Berlin before he committed his fighters to the attack. Galland, in constant contact with Ibel, agreed—although he was beginning to get nervous. If Ibel waited too long, the Me-109s would not reach the Flying Fortresses and Liberators in time to disrupt their bombing runs. This would give the American bombardiers ample time to use their Norden bombsights to great advantage and could be disastrous to the German targets. As the formations neared the Elbe River, Galland contacted Ibel.

"Have you sent your planes up yet?"

Ibel replied that he hadn't. "I need a few minutes more."

His patience paid dividends! Within a matter of minutes Ibel noticed that the plots of the bomber formations being sent to his headquarters by the control center indicated that the American planes were turning to the right.

"It's the Leipzig area," he said. "Not Berlin."

Number Two Division took off immediately, heading for the industrial complex at Leipzig instead of wasting precious fuel and time on a futile flight to the Berlin area. Ten minutes after leaving the field at Stade, Lieutenant Deiter Petz spotted the lead Flying Fortress of the first formation.

"Enemy formation at three o'clock low!"

Colonel William T. Seawell, commanding officer of the Four Hundred First Group, was in the lead Flying Fortress that Petz saw as he led the Me-109s towards the bomber formations heading for Leipzig. The Four Hundred First Group, flying out of a base at Deenethorpe, England, had only started operations in November, 1943, and was the newest of the First Division's groups, but its operational record for the past three months had been excellent. Now, as the lead Flying Fortress turned onto the bombing run from the IP, Seawell was determined that his crews would hit the target despite the imminent attack by the Luftwaffe. Holding the lead B-17 straight and level, so that his bombardier could line up the cross hairs of the Norden bombsight accurately, the colonel warily kept an eye on the enemy fighters approaching from the north. He saw Ibel's Me-109s looking over the lead formation closely, saw them fly parallel a few hundred feet higher than the bombers, and finally saw the enemy fighters bank toward the lead Flying Fortress, his aircraft, to begin their first pass.

"Steady . . . steady . . ." he said calmly over the interphone as the Flying Fortress droned closer and closer to the bomb-release point.

While Seawell braced himself for the exploding shells

he was certain would rip into his plane as the Luftwaffe fighters began firing, Lieutenant Colonel Donald Blakeslee, leading the Three Hundred Fifty-Seventh Fighter Group, was watching the Me-109s. He and the other P-51s of the Three Hundred Fifty-Seventh were at 25,000 feet, and when Blakeslee saw Petz bank his Me-109 towards the Flying Fortress formation, he radioed: "Let's go!"

Leading the P-51s down in a steep dive, he intercepted the Luftwaffe fighters before the Germans could make a successful firing pass on the heavy bombers. Within minutes Mustangs and Messerschmitts were climbing and diving above and below the Flying Fortresses making their bombing run. Seawell's group made one of the most accurate bomb drops of the day and caused severe damage to buildings of the A.T.G. Maschinenbau GmbH plant. Blakeslee's fighter pilots shot down two enemy fighters and destroyed two others during the short melee over the target area. Lieutenant Donald Ross of the Three Hundred Sixty-Third Squadron of the group claimed an Me-109 but was then hit by enemy fire and had to bail out. It was later learned that he was captured and imprisoned by the Germans.

As briefed, Seawell led his formation off the target after the bomb drop in a descending course, taking evasive action at the same time. Ibel's Number Two Division fighters—those that managed to break clear of the Mustangs—gave chase. The deputy lead plane of the Four Hundred First, piloted by Lieutenant A.H. Chapman, had an engine damaged so seriously it had to drop out of formation. True to the name painted on its nose—Battlin' Betty—the crew took the plane down to treetop level in order to avoid as many enemy fighter attacks as possible and started across Germany towards England. The odds against the damaged B-17 getting back to its base were astronomical, but Chapman ignored this fact and, avoiding

106

antiaircraft emplacements as best he could, piloted the aircraft home safely!

Not all the Flying Fortress crews were so lucky, however. One that wasn't was a B-17 of the Three Hundred Fifth Group piloted by Lieutenant William R. Lawley from Alabama. The citation for the Medal of Honor he was awarded for his actions that day details his ordeal clearly:

For conspicuous gallantry and intrepidity in action above and beyond the call of duty, 20 February 1944, while serving as a Pilot of a B-17 aircraft on a heavy bombardment mission over enemy-occupied continental Europe. Coming off the target he was attacked by approximately 20 enemy fighters, shot out of formation and his plane severely crippled. Eight crew members were wounded, the copilot was killed by a 20-mm shell. One engine was on fire, the controls shot away and Lieutenant Lawley seriously and painfully wounded about the face. Forcing the copilot's body off the controls, he brought the plane out of a steep dive, flying with his left hand only. Blood covered the instruments and windshield and visibility was impossible. With a full bomb load the plane was difficult to maneuver and the bombs could not be released because the racks were frozen. After the order to bail out had been given, one of the waist gunners informed the pilot that two crew members were so severely wounded that it would be impossible for them to bail out. With the fire in the engine spreading, the danger of an explosion was imminent. Because of the helpless condition of his wounded crew members Lieutenant Lawley elected to remain with the ship and bring them to safety if it was humanly possible, giving the other crew members the option of bailing out. Enemy fighters again attacked but by using masterful evasive action he managed to lose them. One engine again caught on fire and was extinguished by skillful flying. Lieutenant Lawley remained at his post, refusing first aid until he collapsed from sheer exhaustion caused by loss of blood, shock and the energy he had expended in keeping the plane under control. He was revived by the bombardier and again took over the controls. Coming over the English coast one engine ran out of gasoline and had to be feathered. Another engine started to burn and continued to do so until a successful crash landing was made on a small fighter base. Through his heroism and exceptional flying skill Lieutenant Lawley rendered outstanding distinguished and valorous service to our nation.

The Eighth Air Force had already started to pay the toll for its all-out aerial assault on the German aircraft industry, although the first mission was only hours old.

While Lawley was fighting his epic battle in his crippled B-17 of the Three Hundred Fifth Group, a few miles away another crew had encountered the Me-109s of Ibel's Number Two Division and faced death as a result. In the lonely air battles five and six miles above the terrain, each crew had to survive or die by itself. No one else could get aboard the damaged plane to help out, no mechanic could tell the pilot to pull the crippled heavy bomber over to the side of the road until he repaired the damage caused by the exploding enemy shells.

"You fly as far towards home with what you have left to fly and with the crew members still alive," one B-17 pilot told an inquiring reporter early in the air war. "When you can fly no more, you make your final decision to crash land or bail out ... if you have the time. Depending on what happens next, you either get a pretty medal or a coffin."

On February 20, 1944, a Flying Fortress of the Five Hundred Tenth Bomb Squadron, Three Hundred Fifty-First Group, a B-17 with the name "Mizpah" painted on its nose, went to Leipzig and came home to England, but not all of the crew survived the lonely ordeal. Their story is an example of the love of man for his fellow man and what happens when airmen are forced to decide whether merely to mouth these nice-sounding words or back them up with action.

The Mizpah was no different from hundreds of other B-17s that took part in the first blow of the all-out aerial assault . . . except for Archie Mathies, her flight engineer. Tall and husky with blond hair and blue eyes, Mathies didn't look like the raw, rugged Pennsylvania coal miner he had been before joining the USAAF after graduating from Monongahela High School. After the usual training courses, Mathies headed for England in December, 1943, just in time to take part in Big Week.

In England he met a big four-engined drab-colored Flying Fortress, which he learned to know better than he had ever known his own home in Pennsylvania. At Bovington and later at his base at Glatton, northwest of Cambridge, the sergeant studied and worked on the B-17 until he knew every bolt, fuse, cable, and engine part intimately. When his buddies teased him about the attention he was paying the bomber at the expense of the girls in the surrounding villages, Mathies just patted the side of the Flying Fortress and said, "Someday this big girl will get me a medal." After a conference, during which every crew member had an opportunity to suggest a name for the B-17 Mathies took such good care of, it was decided to name it Mizpah. The mother of pilot Lieutenant Clarence R. Nelson had mentioned the word in a letter to him, remarking that it was a Biblical term meaning, "The Lord watch between me and thee while we are absent one from another."

It proved to be a long separation!

The Mizpah came under attack by Ibel's Messerschmitts in the Leipzig area. Mathies was firing at the attacking Me-109s when he suddenly detected the acrid smell of smoke in the heavy bomber as the plane bounced crazily from the prop wash of the enemy fighters. Without warning the B-17 seemed to stop in midair, remain motionless for a few seconds as though trying to decide what to do next, and then with slow-motion deliberateness it slid off on the left wing and headed straight down through five miles of empty space. Mathies immediately dropped down from the top turret and looked into the cockpit. One glance told him that Ronald E. Bartley, the copilot, was dead. In the left bucket seat, Nelson the pilot, was draped unconscious over the control column. Mizpah was on the loose with no restraining hand to guide her and she was taking full advantage of her freedom.

By the time Mathies extricated himself from his headset, oxygen line, and safety belt, the navigator, Walter E. Truemper, had crawled up through the nose hatchway. Between the two of them they managed to lift the wounded and unconscious pilot from his seat and onto the floor of the cockpit of the diving plane.

Mathies slid into the vacant pilot seat and grabbed the control column with both hands. Using all his strength, the strength his coal-mining labors had developed, the flight engineer finally pulled the damaged B-17 out of its death dive and got it flying straight and level over the German countryside. Immediately the navigator warned the crew to bail out, that both the pilot and copilot were wounded and unconscious, that there was no choice except to abandon the Flying Fortress.

Mathies, however, didn't agree. "Let's try and take the plane home, Lieutenant. Right now she's flying okay. We can bail out later if its necessary."

Truemper didn't look forward to becoming a prisoner of war either and after staring at the snow-covered terrain

110

below for a few seconds he nodded. "I'm game. I'll tell the crew. Those that want to take their chances with us can stay in the plane. The rest can bail out."

The remainder of the crew stayed with Mathies and Truemper as Mizpah began the long trip home. It was a flight that later seemed impossible. Alone, deep in enemy territory, the pilot unconscious, the copilot dead, and the B-17 a flying wreck held together by a few undamaged braces and bolts and piloted by a flight engineer with no previous flying experience, it was an unlikely gamble. Yet, at 1630 hours on the afternoon of February 20, 1944, Mizpah appeared over the airbase at Glatton, England.

"Mayday! Mayday! Glatton this is Mizpah calling!"

In the tower at the Eighth Air Force field everything else was halted at the urgent Mayday call. Colonel Eugene A. Romig, commanding officer of the Three Hundred Fifty First group, looked at the operations officer standing beside him holding a clipboard. "Who is in Mizpah?"

"That is Lieutenant Nelson's plane."

The control-tower operator tried to contact the Flying Fortress but there was no answer. Suddenly another call came from the damaged B-17.

"Mayday, Glatton. Mayday!"

"Go ahead, Mizpah. We receive you loud and clear."

For a moment there was no reply as the big bomber wobbled above the field at less than 1,000 feet altitude. "Tower, this is Sergeant Mathies. I need help."

Colonel Romig looked at the other men in the control tower and saw that they were as puzzled as he was. Why was a sergeant making the radio calls usually made by the pilot or copilot? He walked over and picked up the microphone. "Sergeant, this is Colonel Romig. What is your trouble? Where is Lieutenant Nelson?"

The B-17 had made a wide turn to the right and was now headed back toward the air base. It was low, so low

111

that at a distance it was partially hidden by the trees at the edge of the field.

"Do you hear me, Sergeant?" the colonel asked when there was no reply to his question.

"I hear you colonel but I can't talk right now. I'm trying to get above the trees."

Romig stared at the plane for a moment and then asked, "Who is flying that B-17?"

"I am, Colonel."

For the next few minutes the colonel asked enough questions to discover the situation in the Flying Fortress crossing and recrossing the airbase in an erratic flight pattern above the tower. It was hard for Romig to believe that the sergeant, with the help of Truemper, the navigator, had flown the B-17 to England from Germany—but since the Mizpah was directly overhead at the moment it was obviously a fact.

"Now what do we do, Colonel?"

Romig knew there was only one answer. "I want you to climb to an altitude of three thousand feet. Just take it slow and easy. Listen closely to what I tell you. First, increase the rpm to twenty three hundred."

"No instrument, Colonel."

The colonel grimaced but when he spoke again his voice was cool and collected. "All right, bring the propeller controls forward until they are about an inch from the stop." Turning to the other officers in the room, Romig said, "This boy is in a bad fix."

"Prop controls set."

"Good work. Now check and make sure the mixture controls on the pedestal are in the 'rich' position."

They were. Gradually going over the "before climb" checklist with the sergeant, the colonel prepared the plane for a climb to an altitude of 3,000 feet. It was a long slow ascent. Mathies kept the plane in a wide climbing turn so that he wouldn't lose sight of the field while Romig talked

General James H. Doolittle, who led the Eighth Air Force during the Big Week, February 20 to 25, 1944.

Adolph Galland, General of the Fighters of the German Air Force. At his left is Professor Boemer of the Ministry of Propaganda for Germany.

Left to right, General Doolittle, General Carl Spaatz and Captain Robert Johnson inspecting a bomber station.

Lt. E. M. Gaston and crew of the 401st Bomber Squadron, 91st Bomb Group, 8th Air Force, beside the B-17 Flying Fortress "General Ike."

The Boeing B-17, more popularly known as the Flying Fortress, was the fastest and most heavily armored high altitude bombing plane in the world.

The Republic P-47, the Thunderbolt, was used to protect the B-17s. The German FW-190 was more heavily armed and had a longer range.

This Focke Wulf 190, a single seat fighter, used to defend Germany, was forced down by the RAF, and was undergoing flying tests by the British.

Germany's most successful fighter plane was the Messerschmitt 109, shown here flying low over the English Channel along the chalk cliffs.

2.

3.

4.

A Messerschmitt 110 of Galland's Luftwaffe fighter arm is destroyed during the
violent aerial battles of the big week.

A British fighter pilot who flew escort missions with the American bombers examines the damage to his Hawker Hurricane.

A German Me-109 after a safe return, despite British fire which caused extensive damage.

The RAF bombed Germany at night during the big week. This Hanley-Page Halifax had to crash land when it reached England after its mission.

One of the unique weapons used by Galland was this "Mistel." A pilot in an Me-109 with a Ju-88 mounted above controlled the explosive-laden robot by radio, releasing it near the target area.

The dauntless workhorse of the U.S. air forces in WW II, the P-51 Mustang.

The famed Nazi pursuit plane, Messerschmitt Me-109.
This particular plane has been prepared with a bomb
attached to its belly for a special mission.

to him, and encouraged the sergeant in every way possible. Finally, the colonel estimated that the B-17 was high enough.

"All right, Sergeant, ease the nose of the plane down to the horizon slowly, bring the throttles back about halfway, and reduce the prop controls to the midway position."

It took about five minutes for Mathies to get the B-17 leveled off, and when he had finally accomplished it, Romig called him once again. "Real good. Now I want you to make a wide circle to the south and come back across the field holding the plane as straight and as level as possible. When you cross the edge of the perimeter, order the crew to bail out and then you follow. Is that clear?"

There was no reply from Mathies for several seconds and then he asked the question the colonel had dreaded.

"What about Lieutenant Nelson?"

The answer couldn't be avoided. A decision had to be made. "Has Nelson regained consciousness?" Romig asked.

"No, but I think he is still breathing."

"Think?" There could be no softness now. "Come, Sergeant. Is he or isn't he?"

There was no answer. As the B-17 passed over the field three parachutes blossomed in the sky. The heavy bomber made a slow turn to the left and on the second pass over the runway two more crew men left the doomed aircraft. Patiently the colonel waited for the Mizpah to make the third and final circuit, but instead the plane turned wide of the base.

"All right, Sergeant. It's getting dusk. Come back over the field and bail out."

Mathies' voice was calm as he radioed, "I'm not jumping. I'm not going to leave Lieutenant Nelson up here alone."

The colonel did everything he could to get the sergeant

113

to bail out—threatened, pleaded, frightened—but it was a waste of time. Neither Mathies nor the navigator would bail out and leave their pilot.

"When I get north of the field, have the fire trucks and ambulances ready, Colonel. I'm coming in."

Romig tried one final time to stop the determined sergeant, but Mathies didn't even reply. Slowly, inexorably, the heavy bomber circled around the west side of the air base and banked to the north. At a distance of approximately three miles from the runway, Mathies banked the B-17 again and headed for the runway.

"Wait," Romig radioed. "I'm coming up in another B-17 to help you."

Five minutes later Romig and another pilot took off in a second Flying Fortress, climbed to the same altitude as the Mizpah and flew alongside. Since the sergeant was unsteady on the controls, it was difficult for Romig to fly close to the other Flying Fortress, but even at a distance he could see the white-faced sweating sergeant sitting in the Mizpah's pilot's seat. After establishing radio contact with Mathies with help of the tower, the colonel made one final effort to convince the flight engineer and the navigator to bail out, but it was a futile effort. Mathies and Truemper were determined to land the huge bomber.

"All right," Romig said. "In that case, let's go over the landing checklist item by item."

The colonel made certain that the sergeant understood each item on the checklist and that he complied. When the checklist was finally completed, he ordered Mathies to follow him down, doing exactly what he did and flying at the same speed and altitude.

"When I drop my landing gear, you drop yours. The same with the flaps and everything else. Do you understand?"

The sergeant said that he did and the two Flying Fortresses started a slow descent toward the runway at

114

Glatton. Initially the letdown went very well. Romig led the Mizpah down to traffic-pattern altitude, rolling out on the downwind leg at 1,000 feet above the hangars. While the sergeant's turns were not smooth, at least he kept the big plane out of dangerous attitudes. The wind had increased to between ten and fifteen mph, with gusts to twenty mph, by the time the two B-17s reached the landing pattern. The colonel knew that this would make the actual touchdown more difficult but there was nothing he could do about it. The two aircraft turned ninety degrees to form a base leg, but for the first time Mathies faltered. He didn't recover from the turn quickly enough and nearly hit Romig's B-17. Frightened at the near miss, he banked sharply in the opposite direction and by the time he regained complete control of the Mizpah, he was out of position for a landing attempt.

Realizing that he was making the sergeant nervous in the formation-type landing attempt, the colonel landed his B-17 and hurried back into the tower to try to talk Mathies down safely. On the first attempt, the sergeant allowed the Flying Fortress to get too low too far from the runway, but he managed to climb back to landing-pattern altitude without incident. On the second attempt Romig successfully directed Mathies onto the base leg, but as the sergeant made the final turn to approach the runway he permitted the nose of the bomber to drop too far. Realizing his error, he leveled off, but he was too low and moving too fast by this time. Romig tried to get Mathies to climb back to landing-pattern altitude and start over but the sergeant was too tired, too nervous.

"It's now or never. I can't do any better."

He reduced the power as instructed, but when he dropped the flaps, the officer and enlisted men in the control tower saw the B-17's nose swerve dangerously. Making a low, long approach to the runway, with the B-17, flying a snaky course that had the plane lined up with the runway one moment and not lined up the next, Mathies did the best he could. The tires touched the runway, squealed in protest, and then because of the excessive speed, the B-17 skipped back into the air. The sergeant was too inexperienced to handle the situation, didn't have the coordinated instinct a veteran pilot needed to make the proper correction for such a touchdown. The left wing of the B-17 dropped while the big plane was at the top of a high bounce, dug into the ground beside the runway, and the Flying Fortress did a gigantic cartwheel and crumpled into a mass of flames.

There were no survivors.

February 20, 1944, was the only day in the history of the Eighth Air Force that more than one Medal of Honor was bestowed on its members. Both Mathies and Truemper were posthumously awarded the medal in addition to Lawley. As Doolittle had predicted, the all-out air assault was going to be costly.

Yet overall the Eighth Air Force had surprisingly light losses on the twentieth, compared to the anticipated losses. The Third Division was attacked by only a few Luftwaffe planes during its long mission to Poland, while the First and Second Divisions were harassed mainly in the target area. Twenty-five heavy bombers were lost and four fighters. Compared to the sixty heavy bombers lost on the October 14, 1943 mission to Schweinfurt, the last large-scale attempt by the Eighth Air Force to penetrate deep into Germany, it was an encouraging sign that the P-51s were scaring the Luftwaffe fighters away from the bomber formations or keeping the Me-109s and FW-190s too busy dogfighting to attack the B-17s and B-24s. It was estimated that the German air force lost 153 fighters during the day, but later studies indicated that this figure might have been unintentionally exaggerated.

Every target that was bombed under visual conditions suffered severe damage. The mission caused a loss of slightly more than one month's output at the airframe manufacture and assembly plant at Leipzig. The Erla Maschinenwerke GmbH's main plant at Heiterblick and its assembly plant at Mockau both suffered heavily. Forty-two Me-109s, just completed and sitting on a nearby airfield, were destroyed by the American bombs, as were 450 workers in slit trenches and poorly constructed air-raid shelters provided at Heiterblick. The Germans admitted later that this first blow of Big Week was so effective that Speer and other Third Reich officers decided on a program to immediately disperse the aircraft industry to safer areas, deeper into Germany if possible and underground whenever facilities were available.

On the evening of February 20, 1944, the two protagonists of the air battle, Doolittle and Galland, analyzed the day's mission. Neither was elated, neither was discouraged. They both realized that this was merely the opening round of the main bout. Both still had surprises to introduce into the fight-to-the-finish operation. The consensus of opinion on both sides of the English Channel on the evening of February 20, 1944, was that this initial battle had ended in a draw.

At 2100 hours that night a brief teletype message was sent to all Eighth Air Force installations:

FAVORABLE WEATHER FORECAST FOR TOMORROW. WE WILL FLY ANOTHER MAXIMUM EFFORT MISSION.

8
"ACHTUNG! ACHTUNG!"

At Galland's central combat station, all eyes were on the big frosted-glass panel that would indicate whether any enemy formations were approaching. To the right of the frosted-glass panel were posted aircraft numbers, while on the opposite side was a map showing the entire German territory, including Holland, Belgium, France, and the Channel coast. Any enemy planes penetrating this area would be plotted on the map as soon as the radar operators, men or women at the listening posts, or pilots of German reconnaissance planes reported them. The entire room was filled with the hum of radio equipment, the ringing of telephones, the buzzing of warning signals, and the voices of the personnel.

Suddenly, at a few minutes before 1000 hours on the morning of February 21, 1944, a shrill alarm bell in the control center rang. The officer sitting at the command table of the control center watched the lights on the control panel blink on one by one in the sectors to the west of Germany proper. He knew instantly that the Allied bomber formations were once again heading for the Third Reich. Colonel Otto Heyte had been in various Luftwaffe control centers for so long that he reacted instinctively. Turning to the officer sitting beside him, he asked, "Are the lines clear?"

"*Jawohl.* All direct leads are functioning properly."

In front of Heyte were more than a hundred levers. A

118

light pressure from the colonel on any one of the levers instantly connected him with a telephone in a fighter-control sector. Now, as he watched the lights and plots of the enemy heavy bombers approaching Germany, he prepared to alert the Luftwaffe pilots at the fighter stations—who were waiting for the word from control center to take off. It was a tense moment for the colonel. It was also a tense waiting period for the Luftwaffe pilots. . . .

Lieutenant Bruno Lessing of the Luftwaffe's Number Three Division, stationed at Deelen, sat in the chair in the pilot's lounge and tried to get some rest. He was tired. The Allied operation of the previous day had forced him to fly three missions; and although he had managed to get four hours' sleep on the night of February 20, 1944, he was still weary from the ordeal. He slouched further down in his chair, closed his eyes, and tried to ignore the roar of an engine that a mechanic was testing out on the flight line. Lessing hoped that the weather was bad over the English bases of the American heavy bombers, that the clouds were down to the runway. Not that he was frightened of the B-17s, B-24s, or even the P-51s, but he needed a day off from combat. A man's nerves could stand only so much and then they needed a period of peace and quiet. Perhaps today would be that . . .

The ring of the telephone in the lounge brought him instantly to a straight-up sitting position. He plainly heard the sergeant's voice as he took the message and repeated it for verification.

"Division expects enemy formations over Darleen within the hour. All pilots alerted. Thank you."

There was no need for the sergeant to repeat the message to the pilots in the room, since they had all heard the telephone conversation—but he did anyway. The thirty fliers in the lounge put down their books, gently laid aside their chess boards, or rubbed the sleep from their eyes. They knew it wouldn't be long until the order came for them to take off, so that they could reach a higher altitude than the American heavy bombers before the Allied aircraft reached the Deelen sector. It was standard operating procedure to attack from above, from out of the sun if possible. Lessing buttoned his jacket and studied the chart in front of him at the same time.

"You should know every rivet on the Flying Fortress by now, Bruno," a Luftwaffe Pilot sitting beside him said as he watched the lieutenant stare at the picture and description of the American B-17 heavy bomber. Lessing smiled but said nothing. He had been battling the Allied bombers for more than two years on the Western front, and he knew that the American crews were getting better and better as time passed. The odds of an Me-109 making a pass at an eighteen- or twenty-one-plane formation without getting hit at least once by one of the shells from the machine guns aboard the bombers were getting shorter and shorter. As he read the excerpt from the B-17 pilot's handbook, which Berlin had obtained in some manner and provided to the German fighter pilots, he understood why the odds were changing:

The B-17 is a most effective gun platform. Your gunners belong to one of two distinct categories: turret gunners and flexible gunners. The power turret gunners require many mental and physical qualities similar to what we know as inherent flying ability since the operation of a power turret and gunsight are much like that of airplane flight operation. While flexible gunners do not require the same delicate touch as the turret gunner, they must have a fine sense of timing and be familiar with the rudiments of exterior ballistics.

120

All gunners should be familiar with the coverage area of all gun positions, and be prepared to bring the proper gun to bear as the conditions may warrant. They should be experts in aircraft identification. Where the Speery turret is used, failure to set the target dimension dial properly on the K-type sight will result in miscalculation of range. They must be thoroughly familiar with the Browning aircraft machine gun. They should know how to maintain the guns, how to clear jams and stoppages, and how to harmonize the sights with the guns.

The importance of teamwork cannot be over-emphasized. One poorly trained gunner, or one man not on the alert, can be the weak link as a result of which the entire crew may be lost. Keep the interest of your gunners alive at all times. Any form of competition among the gunners themselves should stimulate interest to a high degree.

Lessing shook his head as he read the excerpt. The American gunners he faced all seemed to be well trained and definitely on the alert. Even when he had made a pass from out of the sun the day before, the top turret gunners had been firing at his Me-109 before he was in range. Six months earlier he would have been able to sneak in and make at least one pass before they had spotted him.

As he lit another cigarette, the German lieutenant stared at a second chart, one that was posted on the wall of the pilot's lounge. It depicted an eighteen-plane formation of American Flying Fortresses, and in the lower-left corner was a photograph of a B-17, with each gun position outlined in red. One look at the red dots was enough to make a Luftwaffe flier shudder. In the nose section, where the bombardier and the navigator performed their duties, were three fifty-caliber machine guns; between the nose section and the bomb bay, on the flight deck directly behind the pilot and copilot, was a Sperry power turret with twin fifty-caliber machine guns; aft of the bomb bay the radio operator had one fifty-caliber machine gun to use for defense; in the bottom of the waist section a Sperry ball-type power turret was installed in the B-17, and it was equipped with two more fifty-caliber machine guns; two flexible fifty-caliber machine guns were located in the waist gunners' compartment, one on each side; and in the extreme end of the fuselage, in the tail gunner's compartment, were two direct-sighted fifty-caliber machine guns.

In addition Lessing was aware that the newer Flying Fortresses also had an electrically operated chin turret equipped with two fifty-caliber machine guns with a hydraulic charging mechanism. The sights were synchronized with the turret-turning mechanism, and this new installation was operated by the bombardier.

On this model there were only two hand-operated machine guns in the nose, instead of three as in the B-17s without the chin turret. This meant that there was a total of twelve or thirteen machine guns on each of the Flying Fortresses, depending on the model, and simple arithmetic told Lessing that an eighteen-plane formation of B-17s had 236 fifty-caliber machine guns ready to fire at attacking fighters! That made the armament on the Me-109, which consisted of two fifteen-millimeter MG 151 cannon and one MK 108 cannon firing through the airscrew boss seem puny. When the American heavy bombers were in their "V" formation, six planes in the lead squadron and six planes each in the high and low squadron flying in position on the lead squadron, the machine guns covered every possible angle from which a Luftwaffe pilot could approach. The lieutenant sighed and closed his eyes. There was no easy way to fight the American formations. None.

The telephone rang a second time. The message was short, decisive:

"All pilots will take off at once!"

Within three minutes Lessing was climbing into the cockpit of his Me-109, and after strapping himself into his parachute harness he started the single Daimler-Benz twelve-cylinder liquid-cooled engine. He taxied into position among the other planes of the Number Three Division, looking skyward every few seconds to make certain that no P-51s of the Eighth Air Force were sweeping the area ahead of the Flying Fortresses. He didn't want to get caught in takeoff position by such an attack because there was no escape in such a situation.

The sky was empty of other aircraft, however, and stayed empty until he was given the signal to take off. Lessing gave the Me-109 full throttle, watching the engine instruments closely as the Daimler-Bentz power plant revved up to 2,800 rpm. When all the needles stayed in the green, he switched his eyes to the runway and ruddered the plane straight as it gained speed.

Two-thirds of the way down the airstrip the Me-109 lifted easily into the air, and Lessing retracted the landing gear quickly in order to reduce the drag and increase his climbing speed. He wanted to get to altitude as soon as possible so he would be in a better attack position when the Flying Fortresses arrived in the Deelen sector.

Momentarily his eyes glanced toward the landing-gear switch in the cockpit, and at that instant there was a violent explosion and his fighter rocked in the resulting concussion. The lieutenant at first thought the blast had originated in his own aircraft, but an immediate check of his instruments gave him no indication of trouble. The Me-109 was still climbing at a fast rate, the air speed was normal, all engine instruments in the green. As he looked out the cockpit canopy to check the nose of the fighter he suddenly saw what had happened. A pall of smoke drifted skyward from the ground directly below him and he realized that the Me-109 that had taken off directly ahead of him had crashed!

There was nothing the lieutenant could do to help the other pilot—and no time, either. He continued to climb on course, following several other Me-109s that were heading for the rendevous altitude of 30,000 feet.

"Ice! All aircraft beware of ice!"

He heard the warning come over the radio and looked out the canopy toward the leading edge of the left wing. Already there was a thick coating of ice on it, which dangerously reduced the efficiency of the wing. At the same time he noticed that his engine was beginning to run rough and realized that his carburetor was icing up also. He flipped on the carburetor heat and put the mixture control in the "rich" position, but there was nothing he could do about the ice on the wings. The controls became more and more sluggish as the ice increased, and Lessing saw one Me-109 pilot completely lose control of his aircraft. The lieutenant checked his parachute harness in case the same thing happened to him. He also checked the outside-temperature instrument on the panel and saw that it read minus four degrees.

"Enemy bombers entering your sector now!"

The radio message from the central control center irritated the lieutenant, who was fighting to survive. It interrupted his thoughts, delayed the decision he had to make. He could either start a descent and hope he reached a warmer temperature and the ice melted off before he got too low to bail out or he could continue to climb and hope he would reach an atmospheric condition in which ice did not form and the ice on the wings would break off. If he went down, the American Flying Fortresses would have one less fighter to oppose them; and Lessing—despite his realization of the danger he faced everytime he attacked an Allied armada such as the one that had just entered his sector—had the fighter-pilot instinct common to fliers in both the Allied and Axis air forces. He wanted to challenge the invading planes and pilots! Consequently he took the more dangerous course and kept climbing.

It was a gamble that paid off for the Luftwaffe pilot. At 21,000 feet he saw chunks of ice begin to break off the wing leading edges, and pieces of the prop ice hammered hard against his cockpit canopy as they dislodged from the whirling propeller. The controls once again felt firm in his hand and the Me-109 responded immediately to his movement of the controls. He was still congratulating himself on his good fortune when he noticed a large group of black spots in the sky far to the west. As he watched the dots they gradually took shape, and he realized it was the lead B-17 group of the Allied armada heading for Germany. Lessing squirmed to a better position in the cockpit and forced his Me-109 ever higher until he was three thousand feet above the oncoming heavy bombers. On all sides of him other Me-109 pilots of Number Three Division were following his procedure—climbing higher, arming their guns, preparing themselves physically and mentally for the first pass against the Flying Fortress formation droning eastward. . . .

At approximately the same time that Lieutenant Lessing of the Luftwaffe had arrived at the pilot's lounge on the Deelen airfield, Major Arthur Bockman had been climbing into a B-17 at a base in England. As a bright green flare arched skyward over the bomber base a few minutes later, Bockman nodded to the pilot of the aircraft.

"Let her roll!"

As commander of the formation for the mission, the major was sitting in the left seat of the lead bomber, where the regular copilot usually sat. It was his responsibility to make certain that the group formed the proper formation, that it left the English coast on time, flew the correct heading, and accomplished the many other details listed in the field order that had come through on the teletype during the early morning hours of February 21, 1944. Now, as Lieutenant William Lewis, the pilot, eased the throttles forward (using differential power on the four engines to keep the thirty-two-ton aircraft on the runway until it gained enough speed to make the rudder effective), he watched the airspeed and called it out to Lewis.

"Airspeed sixty mph ... seventy ... eighty ... red lights!"

Lewis knew the red lights indicated he was running out of runway fast and heaved a sigh of relief a few moments later when the thump, thump of tires on the runway stopped. It meant the bomber was airborne.

"Gear going up."

The lead B-17 was flying, but still so low that the altimeter read zero. At a signal from Lewis, Bockman retarded the throttles until he had thirty-five inches of manifold pressure on the instrument and 2300 rpm for the propellers. At this climbing-power setting, the lieutenant kept the air-speed needle on 140 mph and turned to home in on the splasher radio beacon by using the needle of his radio compass. Suddenly at 3,000 feet Lewis encountered the same problem that the German lieutenant, taking off later from his base in Holland, would encounter—ice! The four engines of the big bomber began to run rough and lose power.

"Better put the carburetor heat on and close the intercoolers," Bockman told him.

At that same moment the waist gunner reported ice building up fast on the wings. The B-17 had a fine de-icer boot system—rubber boots that "breathed" and cracked the ice off before it got too heavy. There was only one trouble: In combat the de-icer boots were removed. Bockman had to make the same decision that Lessing would have to make later: let back down to a lower altitude and try to melt the ice from the wings or keep climbing and hope he could find an altitude where the temperature and humidity were such that ice would not continue to form. With hundreds of other planes milling around at the lower level as they took off and tried to climb to rendevous altitude, Bockman had no desire to start a descent that could easily lead to a midair collision.

"Keep climbing," he ordered, advancing the throttles further and further to keep the air speed at 140 mph.

The altimeter needle passed the 6,000-foot mark before the major saw sunlight beginning to pierce the overcast. Five minutes later the B-17 broke out into clear skies and bright sunshine, which soon melted the ice from the wings. Bockman nodded at the grinning pilot, as relieved as the lieutenant, and then said, "Start circling the splasher beacon at twenty-five thousand feet so the other planes can form on us."

One by one the other B-17s penetrated the overcast, broke out on top and, homing in on the splasher beacon, soon joined with the lead plane. Twenty minutes later Bockman saw that he had all eighteen of his Flying Fortresses in near-perfect formation and at a distance he saw two other eighteen-plane formations flying an intersecting course to join with his own group. He looked at his watch. Five minutes remained before departure time.

As he relaxed and watched the other aircraft joining with his, he wondered how soon it would be before the Germans discovered that another all-out aerial assault was about to begin on their homeland. Bockman didn't know it but Colonel Otto Heyte at the Luftwaffe's central combat station had already been notified that Allied bomber formations were in the air over the United Kingdom! Nor did he know that one minute before he gave the order for the B-17s to stop circling the splasher beacon, where they had joined in formation, Lieutenant Lessing and the other

Me-109 pilots of Number Three Division were already alerted for takeoff at Deelen!

Picking up his microphone, Bockman radioed, "Tighten up the formation. We're on our way."

The trip across the English Channel was uneventful for Bockman and his formation. Just before reaching the enemy coast the P-51s and P-38s assigned to accompany the B-17s on the flight into the target swept in overhead, and the pilots began flying a criss-cross flight pattern above the formation. The sky was cloudless as Bockman's lead group headed inland, and the visibility was excellent. The major could plainly see the hedgerows and fields below; it was a peaceful scene with no hint of conflict. The sun shining through the windshield warmed the cockpit and he had to fight off a sleepy feeling, knowing that it was ridiculous to feel like dozing over enemy territory when all hell might break loose at any second, but he couldn't help it. He reached above his oxygen mask, took off his sunglasses and started to rub his eyes when his earphones suddenly crackled.

"Fighter plane at two o'clock."

Bockman quickly put his sunglasses back on and stared in the direction the gunner had thought he saw a fighter plane. The major couldn't see anything. Perhaps the gunner was nervous, was seeing black dots that weren't in the sky.

"Do you still see the fighter?" he asked over the interphone.

"Roger. It's now at one o'clock and high."

Bockman looked up and was instantly aware that the gunner had not been seeing illusions. There were several black dots in the sky now, and as Bockman watched the dots take shape, he identified the aircraft as Me-109s. While he was staring at the Messerschmitts, Lessing, in the cockpit of his Me-109, was staring at the Flying Fortresses. . . .

"After them!"

The order came through Luftwaffe pilot Lessing's earphones just as he saw his flight leader dip his left wing tip. The German lieutenant checked his guns, adjusted the sights, and peeled off behind the long line of Messerschmitts diving towards the Flying Fortresses. Grasping the stick with both hands, he groped for the triggers with his right thumb and forefinger as his speed increased and the G-forces slammed him back against the seat. To his right, Lessing saw several P-51s trying to intercept the Me-109s, but he knew he would reach the bombers before the Mustangs reached him. He took careful sight on the lead B-17—the bomber from which Bockman was controlling the lead formation—and pressed the triggers. The Me-109 shuddered as the cannons fired and he saw the shells punch holes in the wing of the B-17.

Lessing had only an instant to glance at the bomber before he went roaring through the formation, through the curtain of fifty-caliber machine-gun fire that was aimed at him and the other attacking fighters of Number Three Division. He heard a dull thud as one of the shells penetrated the fuselage of his fighter directly behind the cockpit. But the Messerschmitt didn't even waver as he climbed steeply away from the formation in an effort to get into position for another pass at the heavy bombers.

At that moment, however, the Mustangs caught up to the Me-109s, and the sky became a maelstrom of milling German and American fighters and Flying Fortresses. The radio was overloaded with warnings and shouts of encouragement as the Luftwaffe pilots attempted to elude the P-51s and once again attack the Flying Fortresses. Lessing, with tracers steaming past his Me-109, dove straight down toward the lead B-17 again and made two more hits on the big plane before he was forced to fall back on his old standby for emergencies—a steep corkscrew climb! At the top of the climb, he looked down and saw smoke trailing the lead Flying Fortress and knew that his shells had damaged the plane. Perhaps it would soon go into a spin and crash and he would get credit for another American bomber. If he . . .

Suddenly something hit his right knee a sharp rap. But before he could examine the knee, he was shocked to see the instrument panel disintegrate. Both incidents occurred within a matter of seconds, but it seemed an eternity to the Luftwaffe flier as he sat in the cramped cockpit of the Messerschmitt, five miles above the ground. When he saw the metal covering over the engine begin to tear away, however, and flames appear in front of the cockpit windshield, Lessing went into action. He knew that an American Mustang had caught him at the top of the corkscrew climb and was methodically shooting his Me-109 to pieces. His only hope was to get to the layer of clouds far below before it was too late, before his entire fighter plane was ripped apart. He didn't want to bail out for fear of getting shot, accidentally or on purpose, by the American fighter pilot chasing him. Nosing straight down, Lessing managed to elude the Mustang and get into the clouds. As he dropped below the clouds he saw a highway, quickly oriented himself, and headed in a glide for the airstrip at Deelen.

When he reached the field, however, he discovered that low-flying P-38s were strafing the installation, setting the aircraft parked on the ground on fire, and bombing and shelling the hangars. With his engine dead, Lessing had no choice but to land amidst the fireworks of the enemy attack—and in a miraculous maneuver he did just that. He touched down fast, bounced once, touched down again, and turned the coasting Messerschmitt onto the grass and headed for the bomb shelter on the perimeter of the field.

Braking to a stop in front of the shelter, the lieutenant leaped out of the plane and limped to the shelter as fast as he could. A mechanic helped him the last few yards and he dove headlong into the shelter just as the P-38s roared over again with their machine guns firing. Outside of a slight wound on the knee, Lessing was uninjured and ready to take to the air again the following day. From a peephole in the dugout he stared skyward toward the American bombers disappearing toward Germany and wondered what had happened to the B-17 he had attacked.

Bockman could have answered the German fighter pilot. The number-three engine had been damaged and had caught on fire briefly; but he and Lewis, the pilot, had managed to extinguish the flames. After a brief discussion, Bockman had decided to continue to the target despite the damaged engine, since he was leading the formation. If he abandoned the mission over Holland, it might result in confusion and impair the results of the raid. The Me-110 engine plant at Brunswick was an important target, one that had to be destroyed, and he didn't want to do anything that might cause the mission to fail or even partially fail.

It was a courageous decision but one that nearly cost him and his crew their lives. Just as they reached the IP, the number-three engine that had been damaged by Lessing's cannon shells caught fire a second time. Bockman stared at the flames and wondered if he could get the fire out this time. Seeing Lewis looking nervously at the flames, he said, "It's okay. We'll make the bomb run."

At that moment the navigator called over the interphone that they were at the IP. Bockman heard the bombardier acknowledge the message and notify the pilot that he was taking over control of the plane through his Norden bombsight. The major rested his hands on the control wheel, ready to override the autopilot, which was

131

being controlled by the bombsight in case of trouble, and stared at the flames billowing from the number-three engine. The temptation to cut the engine and feather the propeller was nearly overwhelming, but Bockman didn't want to do anything that would disrupt the bombardier's delicate corrections as they approached the target. All the other planes dropped their bombs in conjunction with the release of the bombs from the lead plane. The target was destroyed or not destroyed depending on the accuracy of the lead bombardier.

"Bombs away!"

The B-17 lurched upward as the 500-pound bombs dropped from the bomb bay. Lewis immediately closed the bomb-bay doors and swung away from the target in a left bank. As he started to drop a thousand feet in altitude as planned, Bockman said, "We'll have to cut number three."

He went through the procedure carefully. Fuel off, propeller to high rpm, throttle open to scavenge the engine and line of gasoline, press the feathering button. Bockman watched as the propeller slowly turned until its sharp edges were facing the airstream and it stopped. He then reached directly in front of his seat, set the fire indicator dial on "right inboard," and pulled the fire-extinguisher handle. The major kept staring at the number-three engine and the flames that were visible under the cowling. And when, after a couple of minutes, the flames did not disappear, he reached forward again and pulled the second—and last—fire-extinguisher charge. There was another agonizing wait, but this time the flames gradually died out and finally disappeared altogether.

"The fire is out," the major said. He looked at the feathered engine, glanced at the air speed, and then studied the formation he was leading. "We're going too slow with the one engine dead, Lieutenant. We'll have to

132

drop out of the formation and let the deputy leader take them home."

Lewis waited until the deputy leader's Flying Fortress was in position to take over the lead and then eased his bomber down and to the left and out of the formation. He reduced the power settings on the three good engines in an effort to keep them from overheating and watched the air-speed needle drop back to 135 mph. At that airspeed it didn't take the formation long to pull away from the crippled B-17. At that moment the odds were very good that Lessing was going to get credit on the Luftwaffe roles for destroying an American Flying Fortress.

Bockman and the crew he was riding with on the second mission of Big Week were combat veterans who were well aware that there were no Sunday rides on a bombing mission. It was a disciplined crew that knew how to fly and fight intelligently. On February 21, 1944, they came home the long hard way—one lone B-17 by itself. Lewis and Bockman took advantage of cloud cover, stayed as low as possible over enemy terrain, and made several detours around cities and other areas where they suspected the Germans would have a strong concentration of antiaircraft guns.

Finally, late in the afternoon, they reached England. They crossed the coast at Great Yarmouth with two engines out—one feathered and another, which had overheated, windmilling. They had lost the second engine one hundred miles before they reached the English Channel, and there was not enough oil pressure remaining to feather it. Even with the two good engines at maximum power Lewis wasn't able to maintain his 500-feet altitude above the English terrain. With the big bomber dropping fifty feet a minute, despite the full power settings, Bockman ordered the crew to their crash-landing positions and at the same time tried to locate the airfield at Horham.

Although he knew the base was in the general area, the major was unable to spot it.

"Horham from Red Leader. Do you read me?"

"Loud and clear, Red Leader."

Bockman was surprised at the quick response.

"Fire a flare, Horham."

A few seconds later a green flare shot skyward a mile to the left. Bockman pointed it out to Lewis, who immediately banked the crippled aircraft toward it.

"Clear the runways, Horham," Bockman radioed. "Red Leader declaring Mayday. We're coming in."

"Runways clear. Ambulances and fire trucks standing by."

The altimeter read 350 feet as Lewis established the downwind leg of the landing pattern. Both remaining engines were pulling maximum power, but the B-17 was still losing altitude and the major began sweating. He knew that the pilot couldn't turn toward the landing strip too soon or he wouldn't have room to land; but if he waited too long, he would be too low to turn and would dig the tip of the 103-foot wing into the trees bordering the field.

Lewis, exhibiting the skill he had learned during his long months of combat, waited until the last possible second and started a shallow turn toward the runway. At a minimum approach speed of 130 mph he called for Bockman to lower the landing gear. As the wheels dropped into the airstream, the Flying Fortress sagged towards the trees below but Lewis managed to clear this last obstacle by holding the nose high and permitting the airspeed to drop to 125 mph. As the big bomber shuddered and threatened to stall because of the low air speed, the lieutenant eased the nose down slightly and called for full flaps.

"Full flaps coming down," Bockman said as he held the switch to the "down" position.

At the same moment, Lewis pulled back the throttles

on the two good engines to keep from losing directional control, rolled in some trim, and felt the heavy bomber drop out from under him. The plane hit on the dirt over-run area in a cloud of dust that hid the B-17 momentarily, bounced gently, and then came down on the hard-sur-faced runway. Very calmly Lewis braked the B-17 to a stop.

"Looks like we're home!"

Bockman nodded and said nothing. He was too damn tired!

The experiences of the German fighter pilot and the American Flying Fortress crew were repeated with slight variations many hundred times that winter day. The Eighth Air Force sent out 924 bombers and 679 fighters on February 21, 1944, of which Bockman, Lewis and his crew were one. Their targets were the two M.I.A.G. fac-tories at Brunswick, which produced component parts for the Me-110, the fighter park at Diepholz, railway yards at Lingen, and German airfields at Hannover, Achmer, and Hopten. Once again, the Fifteenth Air Force could not cooperate. This time it was bad weather over the Fog-gia area that prevented them from taking off.

Doolittle read the reports of the mission late that eve-ning, studied the reconnaissance photographs of the target areas, and was not satisfied. The large air park at Die-pholz had been seriously damaged by Eighth Air Force bombers releasing their high explosives visually; but at Brunswick the results were not so satisfactory. It had been necessary to use the H2X "blind" bombing equipment because of heavy clouds over the Me-110 factories. Un-fortunately most of the bombs had fallen on the city instead of the aircraft factories!

Nineteen American heavy bombers had been lost along with five American fighters. Eighth Air Force crews reported shooting down sixty German fighters. These

135

figures seem to verify that Big Week was not going to cost as many American lives and aircraft as Doolittle had expected. This was one optimistic note to counter the fact that as yet the Luftwaffe was showing no sign of weakening.

Even this small note of optimism was premature!

9
THE THIRD ALERT

Eighth Air Force headquarters at High Wycombe, northwest of London, was a busy place on the evening of February 21, 1944, as Doolittle and his staff evaluated that day's mission and prepared for the next day's. The impressive headquarters building resembled an English castle and prior to the war had been an exclusive girls' school. When the girls moved out to make room for the officers of the Eighth Air Force, they left behind little cards that went unnoticed by the USAAF men assigned the task of preparing the rooms. These cards read: *Please ring bell twice should it become necessary to summon Mistress.* As could be expected, on the first night the USAAF officers slept in High Wycombe, bells were ringing all night. No mistresses showed up that first night; and on the evening of February 21, 1944, a million bells could have rung without a mistress being within ten miles, nor would anyone have laughed at the misconception as they had that initial night. The situation regarding the all-out battle with the Luftwaffe was too serious for any laughter that night at High Wycombe.

While the heavy-bomber losses had been lower than anticipated during the first two missions of the air campaign against the German aircraft industry and the Luftwaffe, Doolittle was still worried. He was aware that there was no appreciable weakening of the Luftwaffe as yet and, as he told some of his staff that night, "Galland will never give up. We will have to be prepared for persistent fighter attacks from his planes until he either has no planes or pilots left to send against us."

It was also obvious to Doolittle that the bombing accuracy would have to improve if the all-out attack were to succeed. It was disappointing to risk the lives of his crews when, because of bad weather, such risks resulted in either misplaced bombs or the bombing of targets of opportunity instead of the primary targets. It seemed that the "blind" bombing tactics that had been developed after a great deal of time and money had been spent were not successful enough for pinpoint bombing. The results at Brunswick—where the bombs had dropped into the city instead of the aircraft factory, which was the impact point on the second mission—verified the conclusion that the H2X technique was satisfactory for area bombing but not the "pickle barrel" accuracy demanded by the USAAF. Doolittle realized that mechanical difficulties, battle damage, losses, crew weariness, illness, and other factors would drain his resources as the week wore on, and he would not be able to send as large a bomber force into Germany as he would like.

If the aim of Big Week—to seriously damage the German aircraft industry and gain air superiority over the Continent—was to be achieved, the Eighth Air Force had to do better than it had the first two days. He knew that the battle was still far from over, that Galland still had the resources and skill to seriously hamper the American heavy bombers from achieving their goal.

Weather reports for February 22, 1944, continued to indicate excellent prospects for visual bombing over many of the important targets in Germany. Krick's unique method of forecasting the weather, while not perfect, was proving fairly accurate and a definite improvement over past forecasts using the more conventional methods. Not only did he predict good weather in many areas of Germany but he also stated that a high-pressure system was moving south in such a manner that two of the top-priority targets—Regensburg and Schweinfurt—were going to be open for visual bombing attacks. In addition it appeared that the weather would also be clear over the Erkner ball-bearing plant near Berlin, which was the second-highest priority target. When Anderson suggested to Doolittle that simultaneous heavy-bomber attacks could be made on all three of these important targets, the Eighth Air Force commander shook his head.

"I don't think it is wise to spread the bombers so thin. It means we will also have to split the fighter escort and this will make our formations too vulnerable to enemy attacks."

The discussion between the two veteran combat airmen lasted nearly an hour with both men and their aides listing the advantages and disadvantages of bombing all three targets on the same day. The main factor in Anderson's favor was the weather. He asked Doolittle during the session, "How many days do we get good weather over all three targets and at the same time have our heavy bombers geared up for an all-out attack? Not very often."

Doolittle had to admit that this was true, but he also pointed out that while good weather was a blessing as far as bombing was concerned, it was a detriment when it came to the big bombers trying to hide from the Luftwaffe fighters. If a B-17 or B-24 was knocked out of formation and had to try and make it back to England by itself, clear skies were a sure death notice since the lone plane had no place to conceal itself when enemy fighters began searching for it.

"This operation can't be based on the safety of a few crews that are unfortunate enough to be forced out of the formation," Anderson said. "We must look at the overall plan and its importance."

Some of the officers at High Wycombe that night had to smile at the general's statement because they remembered the decision Doolittle had been forced to make during his famous raid on Tokyo. When the aircraft carrier carrying his B-25s had been spotted by a Japanese reconnaissance plane, Doolittle had ordered his crews to take off hours earlier than planned despite the fact that he knew they didn't have enough fuel to reach the bases they planned to use for landing after dropping their bombs on Tokyo. There had been no hesitation that day about risking his crews and himself to achieve the aim of the mission. They were certain that he was not hesitating now to save the lives of a few crewmen either.

He wasn't. Doolittle was firmly convinced that the Luftwaffe was still capable of launching devastating attacks against his heavy-bomber formations as they penetrated deep into Germany, and he wanted to send his bomber and fighter escort to the targets as a team, not as individual groups or wings scattered all over the Continent. He finally convinced Anderson and the other officers who were in favor of bombing all three high-priority targets that the relatively light losses suffered by the heavy-bomber forces during the first two missions had been the result of massing his aircraft and not splitting the force until it was near the target area. However, he was forced to compromise to a certain extent in that he agreed to send his bombers to both Schweinfurt and Regensburg even after it was decided not to bomb Erkner. This meant that his formations would still be spread dangerously but not as much as they would have been if Erkner had been included on the bombing agenda.

Good news reached High Wycombe later in the evening when Twining, commander of the Fifteenth Air Force, radioed that he would be able to send a force of heavy bombers from his airfields at Foggia to bomb German targets on February 22, 1944. It was immediately decided that Twining's bombers would attack Regensburg from Italy. This meant that Doolittle's Eighth Air Force bombers would not be divided between the Schweinfurt and Regensburg areas after all, a fact that made him very happy. Instead, Doolittle's task force was assigned targets at Schweinfurt, Gotha, Bernburg, Oschersleben, Ashersleben, and Halberstadt, all of which were close enough together that the Eighth Air Force B-17s and B-24s did not have to split their massed formations until they were in the target area. In addition to the Eighth Air Force aircraft going to these targets in the Schweinfurt area and the Fifteenth Air Force aircraft going to the Regensburg area, a small diversionary force, equipped with radar-jamming equipment, was scheduled to fly to Denmark and attack the Aalborg airfield. It was hoped that by sending this small force to the north that the Luftwaffe would not detect the main force of bombers until it had formed over England.

The Third Division, under the command of gruff Curtis LeMay, was assigned the Schweinfurt target. This was the same unit that had flown to Poland on the first mission of Big Week without fighter escort. It was a well-trained division, one that reflected the never-say-die attitude of LeMay, the general who had developed many of the bombing and formation tactics used by the Eighth Air Force and was destined to go to the Pacific and do the same thing within a few months. LeMay's command headquarters was at Camp Blainey and from there he controlled the Fourth and Thirteenth Wings, which made up the Third Division.

The Fourth Wing was composed of the Ninety-Fourth Group from Bury St. Edmunds and commanded by Colonel Frederick W. Castle, an outstanding flying officer who was later to command the Fourth Wing. Ten months later, on the day before Christmas, 1944, Castle would take over the controls of a burning B-17 on a mission, so that the crew could bail out, and die when the Flying Fortress crashed. He would be posthumously awarded the Medal of Honor. On February 22, 1944, however, as he prepared for the mission to Schweinfurt he was primarily known as one of Eaker's "original seven" who had left the safety of a desk job in Washington to take over control of a combat unit.

The Three Hundred Eighty-Fifth Group also belonged to the Fourth Wing. This unit used the RAF base at Great Ashfield, and was commanded by Colonel Elliot Vandevanter, Jr., a veteran of the first shuttle mission to Regensburg earlier in the war. The Three Hundred Eighty Fifth Group was known as "Van's Valiants." The final group of the Fourth Wing was the Four Hundred Forty-Seventh Group flying out of Rattlesden and commanded by Colonel Hunter Harris, Jr.

The second wing of the Third Division which was scheduled to attack Schweinfurt on February 22, 1944, was the Thirteenth Wing, headquartered at Horham, England, and commanded by Colonel Harold Q. Huglin, who had earlier been CO of the ill-fated One Hundredth Group, which had the dubious claim to fame of having the most spectacular heavy losses at intervals throughout the war than any other bomb group in the USAAF. The One Hundredth was a unit of the Thirteenth Wing and flew from Thorpe Abbots. At the time of Big Week the "Bloody Hundredth," as this group was known, was commanded by Colonel Neil B. Harding, a graduate of West Point and a famed football coach. "Chick" Harding had been sent to the One Hundredth Group at a time when its morale was at the lowest ebb and its losses at the highest mark in the Eighth Air Force; and now, in the midst of Big Week, he was determined that the "Bloody Hundredth" would handle its assignment successfully.

The Ninety-Fifth Group at Horham, commanded by Colonel John K. Gerhart, had been a part of the Eighth

142

Air Force since May, 1943, had already been awarded three Distinguished Unit Citations and was destined a month later to be the first American bomb group to bomb Berlin. Gerhart was one of the original officers of the Eighth Air Force and had been sent to the Ninety-Fifth Group after this unit had experienced several tragedies that threatened its future value to the Eight Air Force. Preparing for a mission while at the English base at Alconbury, one of the Ninety-Fifth Group's Flying Fortresses loaded with bombs exploded, and nineteen airmen and officers were killed and twenty more seriously injured. A short time later, the Ninety-Fifth Group went to Kiel, led by General Nathan Bedford Forrest, who wanted to gain combat experience prior to taking command of a new wing. The group had no sooner reached the enemy coast than it was attacked by the Luftwaffe. The general's plane and seven other Flying Fortresses were shot down before the group even reached the target, and only six of the Ninety-Fifth Group's task force returned to England. Gerhart and the Ninety-Fifth Group had also flown the tragic Schweinfurt mission of October 14, 1943, so he was well aware of what faced him and his men on the morning of February 22, 1944, as they prepared to take off for Schweinfurt again.

The Three Hundred Ninetieth Group completed the organizational setup of the Thirteenth Wing. The B-17s of this group, identified by the "J" in the square painted on the tail, used the former RAF base at Framlingham and was led by Colonel Edgar M. Wittan. This group had been bombing enemy targets since August, 1943, and had gone with the Ninety-Fifth Group to Schweinfurt the previous October, for which it had been awarded the Distinguished Unit Citation.

When the Third Division air crews and their commanders were awakened on the morning of February 22,

1944, long before dawn, the first thing most of them did after crawling out from under the heavy covers was to look out the windows at the sky. Even in the blackness of the English countryside it didn't take these combat veterans long to discover that the clouds were hanging extremely low over the airfields. What these fliers were discovering at this time had been known for hours by many of the officers and enlisted men responsible for the planning of the mission.

At the Ninety-Fifth Group at Horham, for example, while Gene Manson and his crew slept, handsome Colonel Gerhart, commanding officer of the group, had been working in the intelligence room for hours. Large maps of the fighting fronts were pinned to the walls of the room and colored markings indicated the important targets in Germany and information about them. In the center of the room was a long, well-polished table around which were eight comfortable leather chairs. In the corner was a radio emitting the soft, slow music that was a speciality of the British Broadcasting System.

With Gerhart in the intelligence room was Major F.J. "Jiggs" Donohue, chief of the group's intelligence section; Captain Wayne Fitzgerald, the group bombardier and Captain Ellis B. Scripture, the group navigator. Gerhart was fond of saying, "If you can't find the target or if you can't hit it after you do find it, why fly the mission?" That was the reason Fitzgerald and Scripture took such an important part in the preliminary planning. When the field order arrived at midnight over the teletype, Gerhart studied it closely, not wanting to miss any of the important details that might mean the difference between success and failure. About this time a short, red-haired lieutenant colonel walked into the intelligence room and also studied the field order. David T. McKnight, who had formerly flown with the RCAF, was the air executive and one of the best-liked officers in the Eighth Air Force.

The field order included the familiar information: the target (in code), the bomb load, the number of aircraft to be dispatched, engineering and communications details, specifications for intelligence, aerial camera installations, the zero hour, and many other facts that were required to coordinate the planned attack. From this information, the officers in the intelligence room at the Ninety-Fifth Group figured out the briefing time, the taxi time, and take off time so that the B-17s of the group would be at the assembly point in formation at the appointed hour to join with the other groups of the Thirteenth Wing.

In group operations, Lieutenant Colonel Harry Mumford, the Group Operations Officer, plotted a schematic diagram of the Ninety Fifth Group formation on the wall. The number of each plane in each position and the name of the pilot was listed. Flying Fortresses that were reported unfit for the next morning's mission were scratched and other numbers put in their places. Mumford was in contact with each of the four squadron operation rooms, and one of his aides telephoned the names of the crews scheduled to fly the mission to each of the squadrons. Briefing time was relayed at the same time. Donohue, the S-2 officer, was busy with his many prebriefing tasks. Required maps were prepared for the flight, briefing information was collected, especially the location of the many flak areas enroute and the Luftwaffe fighter units based along the proposed route to the target and material about the target itself, so that Donohue could orient the crews and give them a picture of its place in the general campaign. It was also his responsibility to have the escape kits prepared for the crews in the event of their being forced down in enemy territory.

While this multitude of tasks were being accomplished in the various buildings of the Ninety Fifth Group during the long night and while the combat crews were still sleeping, many other men were busy out on the flight line. Fuel

145

and bomb loads were determined from the field order, and within minutes huge gas trucks rumbled from one hardstand to another hardstand, pumping gas into the B-17s. Ordnance delivered the required high-explosive or incendiary bombs from the bomb dump at the edge of the airfield, and armorers loaded them on the aircraft. These same armorers checked all the guns and ammunition on each Flying Fortress so that no crew would later be without means to protect themselves when the inevitable German fighters attacked their formation. Aerial cameras were tested before being loaded on designated planes. Photographs of the bombed target were an important part of the intelligence required for future missions, and a nonoperating camera could be costly. The Norden bombsight was preflighted and carried to the B-17s. Finally all the preflight preparations were completed and the men on the line returned to their huts for some rest, knowing that if the weather prevented takeoff the next morning, all their hard work was in vain and they would have to unload the equipment they had just loaded on the aircraft. They were hoping the weather held up.

At 0410 hours, however, approximately 180 combat crew men weren't nearly as enthusiastic about having good weather as the ground crews. They were abruptly awakened by a voice bellowing over the public address system: "Attention all combat crews! Attention all combat crews! Breakfast until 0500. Breakfast until 0500. Briefing at 0515. Briefing at 0515."

The journey from the sack to the parachute was about the most unpleasant aspect of the entire mission for men such as Gene Manson and other pilots, navigators, bombardiers, and gunners of the Ninety Fifth Group scheduled for the day's mission. The wet chill of an early winter morning in England had no equal for putting a man in a black mood, especially when he knew that within a few hours he would be a thirty thousand feet over Germany under attack from the ground guns and enemy fighters!

After getting dressed Manson and the other officers in his hut stepped outside, where a half-ton covered truck was waiting to take them to the mess hall. The men assigned to fly the mission were given fresh eggs for breakfast instead of powdered eggs—"a sort of last meal type of thing," one gunner said—and usually consumed at least one cup of hot coffee to try and warm their shivering bodies.

Once again it was outside to the waiting truck, which took them to the briefing room where Donohue, Fitzgerald, Scripture, Mumford, and McKnight each spoke to the crews about the mission, giving them the information for which they were responsible. Usually the CO, Colonel Gerhart, made a short speech in an effort to make the apprehensive and often frightened crew men aware of the importance of the mission they were about to embark upon and the efforts that had been made to safeguard them in everyway possible. At the same time he knew, and the crews knew, that there really was no way to guarantee their safety, that Lady Luck, skill, and gut-courage would tell whether they returned to Horham that night or stayed in Germany dead or alive.

At the aircraft, the crews checked their B-17s closely, using flashlights and trying to keep the beams covered as much as possible. A favorite German trick was to send several Ju-88s over the American bases before dawn to bomb the crews and aircraft slated for a mission. Since the beam from a flashlight was clearly visible from the air, many of the German pilots "homed in" on the heavy-bomber bases by watching for these tell-tale beams of light.

The pilots made certain that each member of the crew checked his individual station and preflighted the equipment at that station. A failure of an oxygen outlet, for example, could mean death within minutes to a man at thirty thousand feet unless help was forthcoming; and in the confusion and terror of an enemy fighter attack, help was often delayed or nonexistent. Machine guns that would not fire left that area of a heavy bomber unprotected and could mean the difference between life and death for the entire crew. Faulty navigational equipment was responsible for the loss of many Flying Fortress crews who had tried to come home alone after dropping out of formation because of damage to their aircraft. When a B-17 ran out of fuel, that was exactly where the crew had to get out or crash land, and if the navigator erred and the aircraft were still over enemy territory, another blank appeared on the squadron crew list the following morning in England.

Finally all was ready. Manson, carrying his parachute pack, climbed into B-17 "273" and walked through the waist gunner's compartment, through the bomb bay, ducked around the upper turret mechanism and slid into the left seat in the cockpit. He made certain that he placed his parachute pack directly under the seat within easy reach. If he needed it, there would be no time to start hunting for the pack. Once he was comfortable in the seat, he buckled his seat belt, made the necessary adjustments so that his feet rested easily on the rudder pedals, and put on his earphones. Looking out the cockpit window at the low-hanging clouds, Manson felt certain that the mission would be scrubbed, that within the next hour he would be back in his warm bed with nothing to do all day but sleep, eat, and rest.

Doolittle in the underground command room at High Wycombe was also dubious that the mission could be launched. As he studied the latest weather report, he knew that hundreds of B-17s and B-24s and countless fighter planes were poised at the various airfields in the midlands of England waiting for his decision. It was a tough decision to make. If he ordered the hundreds of heavy bombers to take off into the clouds, there was the inherent danger of midair collision if one or more of the pilots strayed from their course while climbing to altitude. Perhaps it wouldn't even be pilot error, it might be a faulty instrument; but regardless of the cause, sure death would be the result. He knew that he could lose a dozen bombers under the circumstances. Yet he also knew that it was a vitally important mission scheduled for the day, one that could have an important bearing on the forthcoming invasion of the Continent.

"General, here is a message from a British reconnaissance plane."

Doolittle took the piece of paper and studied it for a moment. The RAF reconnaissance pilot, flying at 38,000 feet over Germany, had reported that all of Germany was clear!

"Launch the mission!" Doolittle ordered.

At Horham the order was received ten minutes prior to the scheduled takeoff time. In the control tower Captain John Rumisek counted the minutes, then the seconds, and at the precise instant ordered, "Green flare!"

The colorful flare shot skyward from the control tower in a graceful arc, leaving a greenish trail in the clouds that was plainly visible to every pilot on the field. Manson, seeing the flare that signaled the mission was still on, nodded to his copilot. "Let's start engines."

Within minutes the countryside bordering the airfield at Horham shook from the incessant roar of the 1000-horsepower engines of the Flying Fortresses. The English inhabitants of the homes near the perimeter of the base were shaken from sleep and knew that the Yanks were going out to bomb the Germans again. Manson, after getting the four engines of "273" running and checked, watched for the next green flare, which would signal that it was time to taxi to takeoff position. Since he was leading

149

the high squadron, he knew that he followed the B-17 on his left which was the Number 6 plane in the lead squadron. If the sequence were botched on the ground, it made it much more difficult to form later in the air so Manson didn't take his eyes from the area near the tower where he expected to see the next flare.

"Green flare," the copilot called at the same instant that Manson saw it shoot upward into the clouds.

"Roger."

He immediately switched his eyes to the B-17 on his left, hoping that the pilot of that plane would taxi in the right sequence. Three minutes later the Number 6 plane of the lead squadron began moving from its hardstand, and Manson eased the four throttles of his plane forward and released the brakes. The big bomber moved easily out of the hardstand and joined the single line of B-17s heading for the takeoff runway.

"Watch the edge of the taxi strip," he warned the copilot. Manson didn't want to drop a wheel of the bomber off the hard surface of the taxi strip into the mud and get stuck. If he did, he would not only delay his own takeoff but he would block all the B-17s in the line behind him. Controlling the heavy bomber with the brakes and use of differential throttle, Manson successfully maneuvered the big plane to takeoff position. As he waited for the tower-control officer to clear him for the takeoff run, he stared at the clouds.

"I'll make this one on the instruments. You keep me on the runway," he told his copilot, who nodded that he understood.

"Okay, 273, cleared to go."

"Roger, 273 taking off."

Manson eased the four throttles forward all the way as he held the brakes. The B-17 shook and vibrated as the engines tried to pull it forward, and when he finally released the brakes, the big plane leaped ahead so fast it slammed him hard against the back of the pilot seat. Watching the air speed, Manson saw the needle move from zero to eighty, ninety-five, one hundred mph, and he eased back on the control column. Immediately the thud of the tires against the rough spots in the runway quieted and he knew that the B-17 was airborne. A moment later the copilot verified that the bomber was off the ground.

"Roger," Manson said, not taking his eyes from the instrument panel. "Gear up."

As soon as the altimeter read 500 feet and the air speed reached 140 mph, Manson banked the B-17 into a slow turn toward the splasher beacon assigned to the Ninety-Fifth Group to help the pilots form their combat "box" for the trip to Germany. He kept the plane climbing at a steady rate of 500 feet per minute as he flew directly towards the radio beam of the splasher beacon, knowing that somewhere in the clouds hundreds of other B-17s were also climbing to altitude. He hoped that all the pilots stayed on the course they were ordered to fly. If not . . .

10
THE FIASCO

Manson's crew from the Ninety-Fifth Group, flying in "273," was one of 466 American heavy bombers dispatched by the Eighth Air Force from English airfields on February 22, 1944. In addition the Fifteenth Air Force in Italy sent a force of 183 heavy bombers to Regensburg. All the pilots and their crews experienced much the same action as those at the Ninety-Fifth Group that morning, and when Doolittle finally gave the order to launch the mission despite the bad weather over the United Kingdom, the fliers in the left seats of the Flying Fortresses were all just apprehensive as Manson.

An instrument takeoff required skill and experience and practice. Not all the B-17 pilots attached to the Eighth Air Force were skilled instrument pilots, regardless of the fact that they had all been required to pass an instrument flight and written examination in the States before entering combat. In early 1944 the need for bomber pilots was great, and many of the pilots passed the flight examination because of this need, not because of their proficiency. There was no question that they had received the proper instrument training and had received the necessary total hours of instrument time in the air, but that still did not make them instrument pilots. Yet it was unthinkable for an instructor to fail an otherwise qualified pilot in early 1944 simply because he was not an outstanding instrument pilot—and he seldom did!

Consequently, when the B-17s of the Third Division took off on the morning of February 22, 1944, and disappeared at one-minute intervals into the low-hanging clouds, a disastrous fiasco was in the making. The procedure used by the Eighth Air Force during instrument weather—when it was necessary that each bomber climb individually to an altitude above the clouds that permitted the formations to assemble in clear skies—was based on the use of radio beacons, commonly known as splasher beacons. This was a single radio beam transmitted perpendicularly into the air, around which the aircraft of one group would circle at a definite air speed and rate of climb until finally the bomber broke through the top of the clouds into the clear.

Each bomber took off one minute behind the bomber ahead. And *if* this interval was maintained and *if* each pilot maintained the proper air speed and rate of climb designated prior to takeoff and *if* icing or mechanical failure did not force him to alter his plans enroute to the top of the overcast, then everything was fine. However, when several hundred bombers were hidden in a thick layer of clouds, their pilots unable to see one another, unforeseen developments always caused trouble—and death. February 22, 1944, was no exception.

Shortly after takeoff that morning one B-17 pilot of the Third Division lost an engine while he was attempting to follow the restricted flight pattern given to him at briefing. His air speed immediately dropped ten miles slower than it should have been, and in order to keep from stalling his bomb-loaded Flying Fortress and killing everyone aboard, he eased the nose of the big plane down to regain some of the much-needed air speed. This, of course, cut his rate of climb, which was supposed to be 500 feet per minute, to zero. In fact, the bomber lost 200 feet before the pilot could get the engine feathered, increase power on the other three engines, trim the aircraft for climb at the altered power settings, and once again follow the intended flight pattern. The one-minute gap and 500 feet of altitude that supposedly separated him from the B-17 following his bomber was now cut to zero, but for a few minutes Lady Luck kept the two aircraft apart in the clouds.

Neither pilot realized that the other B-17 was within fifty feet of his own bomber . . . not until it was too late! When one Flying Fortress suddenly appeared in the overcast like a gray apparition heading directly toward the second Flying Fortress, there was barely time for a waist gunner to scream before the two aircraft collided. Wings locked, both planes fell to the ground killing all aboard.

This was only the beginning of a tragic day. As the two heavy bombers fell from the sky they narrowly missed several other B-17s climbing through the overcast behind them. One startled pilot, seeing the two B-17s locked together drop past the nose of his own aircraft almost within reaching distance, immediately changed his course a few degrees and brushed against the wingtip of a second B-17 that had also changed its flight path a few seconds earlier. Fortunately there was only minor damage to these two aircraft and both pilots made the dangerous descent through the overcast successfully and crash landed in the midlands with no loss of life.

By this time the heavy bombers of the Third Division were climbing individually with no set pattern. Some of the pilots had been forced to alter their rate of climb because of the midair collision; others were encountering ice and couldn't maintain the briefed rate of climb; a few had hit the panic button and were climbing at full power and maximum rate of climb in a desperate effort to reach the clear sky above the overcast; and some of the frightened pilots had aborted the climb entirely and were descending through the maze of climbing B-17s, making a dangerous procedure at its best much more hazardous for those fliers still trying to maintain the proper course, airspeed and rate of climb. It was obvious that the Third Division was in trouble.

LeMay was alerted to the situation at the Camp Blainey, headquarters of the division. Monitoring radio messages being transmitted by the pilots of the Third Division, the cigar-smoking LeMay recognized tragedy in the making. Many of the voices indicated the confusion and fright of the pilots. Other calls made it obvious that the fliers who were trying to maintain order were angry, and he knew that an angry pilot was often as dangerous to others in the sky as a scared pilot. Several times the colonel tried to regain control of the hundreds of bombers lost in the clouds by giving orders over the radio; but it was impossible. The pilots were either not listening or did not respond to the orders, owing to the stress of the situation. After several additional reports of midair collisions, LeMay knew he had no choice but to abandon the mission.

"Recall the Third Division planes," he ordered.

He knew that he was justified in his decision, that the division could never assemble enough aircraft in time to follow the field-order sequence. If the division left England late because of trouble assembling its formations, it would not meet its fighter escort at the proper time and this could lead to disaster over enemy territory. It was a hazardous mission under any circumstances, but to start such a mission late, with only a small percentage of its aircraft intact in the "box," was foolhardy. Giving orders for the heavy bombers above the clouds to stay at altitude in the clear sky until told to descend, LeMay directed the planes still in the overcast to start to let down at 500 feet per minute when given the signal over the radio. In this manner he hoped to avoid any further midair collisions.

When Doolittle received the word that LeMay had decided to recall the planes of the Third Division, he shook his head in frustration. He knew that the colonel was probably justified under the circumstances but his move jeopardized the aircraft of the First and Second Divisions and the heavy bombers of the Fifteenth Air Force. The Luftwaffe would be able to concentrate on the two remaining divisions of the Eighth Air Force and this could be disastrous. Yet the importance of the mission prohibited a general recall.

"Inform the First and Second Division commanders of the situation," the general said as he continued to study the map in front of him.

The B-24s of the Second Division were scheduled to attack the Me-110 factories at Gotha and dispatched nine groups of bombers on the morning of February 22, 1944. The Second Wing of the division, composed of the Three Hundred Eighty-Ninth, Four Hundred Forty-Fifth, and Four Hundred Fifty-Third Groups, was destined to lead the ill-fated mission. The Three Hundred Eighty-Ninth, known as the "Sky Scorpions" and flying Liberators with a large "C" in a white circle on the tail, had participated in the famed Ploesti low-level raid of August 1, 1943, and received a Distinguished Unit Citation. One member, Lloyd H. Hughes was awarded the Medal of Honor for his part in the mission. Commanded by Colonel Milton W. Arnold and flying from a base at Hethel, England, the Three Hundred Eighty-Ninth was no newcomer to combat, but the veteran crews would need all their experience on this mission if they were to survive.

Flying with this group was the Four Hundred Forty-Fifth Group, under the command of Colonel Robert H. Terrill from a field near Tibenham, England. While this unit did not have as much experience as the "Sky Scorpions," its crews had been to Kiel, Ludwigshafen, Munich, and other targets that made veterans out of newcomers real fast. The third group of the Second Wing, the Four Hundred Fifty-Third at Old Buckenham, had flown its first combat mission only seventeen days earlier, but its commander, Colonel Joseph A. Miller, was determined

156

that his unit would handle its responsibility just as well as the more experienced groups. The wing commander was Brigadier General Edward J. Timberlake, Jr., whose early group of B-17s became famous during the pioneering days of the Eighth Air Force as "Ted's Flying Circus."

Colonel Jack W. Wood's Twentieth Wing was composed of the Ninety Third, Four Hundred Forty-Sixth, and Four Hundred Forty-Eighth Groups on February 22, 1944, and all three units were scheduled for the mission to Gotha. Wood had led one of the heavy-bomber groups on the Ploesti raid and was well aware of what was expected of his crews during Big Week. Flying from a base at Hardwick, England, and commanded by Colonel Leland G. Fiegel, the Ninety Third Group joined the formations of the "Bungay Buckeroos," the Four Hundred Forty-Sixth Group, commanded by Colonel Jacob J. Brogger and based at Flixton, and Colonel James M. Thompson's Four Hundred Forty-Eighth Group from Seething.

The third wing of the Second Division, the Fourteenth, headed by Brigadier General Leon W. Johnson, a Medal of Honor recipient for his heroism during the Ploesti mission, dispatched two groups on February 22, 1944, to bomb the Messerschmitt plants at Gotha. The Forty Fourth Group had already received Distinguished Unit Citations for missions to Kiel and Ploesti in 1943 and was well prepared for the Big Week ordeal. Commanded by Colonel Frederick R. Dent, the Forty-Fourth used a former RAF base at Shipham. The Three Hundred Ninety-Second Group had begun flying combat missions in September, 1943, from Wendling, England, under the watchful eye of its commander Colonel Irvine A. Rendle, and its crews were accustomed to the flak and fighters that were a part of missions over Germany. They were accustomed to them, that is, as well as any man ever could become accustomed to such dealers of death.

The importance of the Second Division increased when

word was received that LeMay had recalled the aircraft of the Third Division. The German aircraft plants at Gotha were a prime target, and it was imperative that the production facilities by destroyed. However, Major General James P. Hodges Second Division could not expect any help from LeMay's B-17s, nor could they depend on the Third Division diverting any of the German fighters from their own formations.

Initially the Second Division fared well despite the bad weather over their bases. The planes of the eight groups climbed through the thick overcast without incident and broke into the clear skies prepared to assemble into formation. The aircraft of the Third Division, however, were scattered all over the area waiting for orders to descend back down through the clouds whenever they received the signal, and these B-17s interfered with the B-24s attempting to assemble. By the time the Second Division was supposed to leave the coast of England and head for the Continent, several of the groups still were not formed into their combat boxes properly, and only one wing had been assembled.

Despite being badly strung out, the Second Division left England at the appointed time, but over the Channel it became apparent that the task force was not in proper formation to attack the assigned targets at Gotha. The Luftwaffe would destroy a large percentage of the bombers if the boxes were not tightened up. A final attempt was made to get the groups into better wing formations and the wings moved closer together as the heavy bombers of the Second Division flew inland from the Channel; but it was a failure and Hodges, like LeMay, decided to recall his planes.

A few of the B-24s searched for targets of opportunity after the recall from the main effort and dropped their bombs on these secondary aiming points, mainly to get rid of them before returning to their bases in England and landing. Unfortunately one Liberator group accidently bombed Nijmegen in Holland, thinking it was a German town, and killed 200 Dutch civilians. Another B-24, attempting to make an approach to the English airfield at Tibenham, accidently released a high explosive bomb, which killed two servicemen and a woman.

With the Second and Third Divisions both recalled, only four combat wings of the First Division, which had been scheduled to bomb Oschersleben, Halberstadt, Bernburg, and Aschersleben, remained airborne and on course for Germany, a total of 289 heavy bombers. Major General Robert B. Williams, who had led a force of 217 bombers to Schweinfurt in August, 1943, in a raid that had nearly cost him his life, commanded the First Division in February, 1944. His division consisted of the First, Fortieth, Forty-First, and Ninety-Fourth Wings at the time, all combat-tested outfits with a large percentage of experienced crews.

The First Wing dated from the Lorraine, St. Michel, and Meuse-Argonne campaigns of World War I and had been in action in England since August, 1942. The roll call of its former commanders while the wing was a part of the Eighth Air Force sounded like a Who's Who of distinguished USAAF officers—Brigadier General Newton Longfellow, Brigadier General Laurence S. Kuter, Brigadier General Haywood S. Hansell, and Brigadier Frank A. Armstrong—and in February, 1944, it was commanded by another such officer, Brigadier General William M. Gross.

His headquarters was at Alconbury, England, from where he directed the Ninety-First and Three Hundred Eighty-First Groups. The Ninety-First had been in combat since November, 1942, and had first penetrated Germany in January, 1943, more than a year before Big Week, when it attacked the navy yard at Wilhelmshaven. Commanded by Colonel Claude E. Putnam, the group flew from the airfield at Bassingbourn, England. Putnam, then a major and executive officer of the group, had been in the lead plane of the first American Flying Fortress formation to bomb Germany in World War II. Flying with the Ninety-First Group was the Three Hundred Eighty-First Group, another veteran outfit, which was commanded by Colonel Harry P. Leber.

The Fortieth Wing of the First Division was headquartered at Thurleigh, England, and was led by Brigadier General Howard M. Turner, who had gained his initial combat experience the hard way with the ill-fated "Bloody Hundredth." Turner had the famed Three Hundred Fifth, the Three Hundred Sixth, and the Ninety-Second Groups in his wing. The Three Hundred Fifth, known as the "Can Do" outfit, was the group originally commanded by LeMay and under him pioneered many formation and bombing procedures that later became standard operating procedure in the Eighth Air Force. It was also the group to which William R. Lawley belonged, the pilot who was awarded the Medal of Honor for his heroic action on the first mission of Big Week, February 20, 1944.

The group with the white "H" in the black triangle painted on the tail section of their Flying Fortresses, which always flew with the Three Hundred Fifth, was the Three Hundred Sixth Group out of Thurleigh, England, commanded by Colonel George L. Robinson, who had led many task forces to Germany during the early months of the air war.

The third group of the Fortieth Wing was the Ninety-Second Group, known throughout England as "Fame's Favoured Few" because those crewmen of this, the oldest unit of the Eighth Air Force, who still survived in February, 1944, had been "favored." Flying from the base at Podington and commanded by Lieutenant Colonel William M. Reid, the Ninety-Second was one of the first groups in tight formation on the Twenty-Second, the day of the third Big Week mission.

The Three Hundred Third, the Three Hundred Seventy-Ninth, and the Three Hundred Eighty-Fourth Groups composed the Forty-First Wing of the First Division, a wing headquartered at Molesworth, England, whose planes and crews flew under the watchful eye of Brigadier General Robert F. Travis. Travis knew exactly what his men faced on the morning of February 22, 1944, as they prepared to attack the German aircraft plants in Germany. On January 11, 1944—a little over a month earlier—he had personally led the First Division to Oschersleben's FW-109 factory in what was a preview of the third mission of Big Week.

Leading the Flying Fortresses in a bomber named "The Eight Ball," Travis found himself behind exactly that when the Second and Third Divisions were recalled because of bad weather at a time when his own division was within 100 miles of the target. Only one squadron of fighter escort was able to penetrate the clouds over the Continent and rendezvous with his formations, and fewer than fifty Mustangs arrived in the target area at the same time as the horde of Luftwaffe fighters that was waiting for Travis' bombers. Altogether thirty-four heavy bombers and H2X Pathfinder planes were shot down, but Travis and the pilot of "The Eight Ball," Lieutenant William Calhoun, successfully brought their plane home safely.

Calhoun was a member of the Three Hundred Third Group, the "Hell's Angels," which was also based at Molesworth. This unit was commanded by Colonel Kermit D. Stevens. Colonel Maurice A. Preston's Three Hundred Seventy-Ninth Group from Kimbolton and Colonel Dale R. Smith's Three Hundred Eighty-Fourth Group out of Grafton Underwood were the two groups that always flew formation with the Three Hundred Third in the Forty-First Wing combat box.

The Ninety-Fourth Wing had one group, the Four Hundred Fifty-Seventh, commanded by Colonel James R. Luper, which flew its first mission on February 21, 1944, the beginning day of Big Week—and the crew men thought that this rugged raid deep into Germany was the normal mission. This new outfit was based at Glatton and flew with the more experienced Four Hundred First and Three Hundred Fifty-First Groups. Colonel Harold W. Bowman's Four Hundred First Group from Deenethorpe, England, had been flying combat with the Eighth Air Force since the previous November and had the second-best rating for bombing accuracy of all the groups in England. The Three Hundred Fifty-First was the group chosen by Clark Gable when he flew with the Eighth Air Force, but it certainly wasn't because Colonel Eugene A. Romig's outfit flew the milk runs. They didn't. In fact the Three Hundred Fifty-First had lost its former commander, Colonel William A. Hatcher, Jr., to enemy action in December, 1943. His bomber had failed to return to the home base at Polebrook.

The First Division heavy bombers had been successful in forming their combat boxes over England, while the Second and Third Divisions had not been able to do so; but as the B-17s flew towards their targets they encountered more and more clouds. The overcast extended much further into Europe than had been anticipated and, more serious, was much higher than predicted. As long as the Flying Fortresses could stay in tight formation and climb over the tops of the clouds, they could protect each other from enemy attacks and obtain better cover from the escorting American fighters.

But it soon became apparent that this was not possible. The wings had to break up, and this made them vulnerable to the Luftwaffe, exactly what Galland had been waiting for so long. The few B-17s that had been dispatched by the First Division's Ninety-Second Group to bomb the airfield at Aalborg, Denmark, as a diversion in hopes of luring some German fighter aircraft to the north and the Fifteenth Air Force coming from the Italian bases in the south failed to draw off the main Luftwaffe force from the First Division heavy bombers heading for Oschersleben, Halberstadt, Bernburg, and Aschersleben in central Germany.

The Three Hundred Sixth Group, however ignored the clouds and remained on course for their primary target, the Junkers plant at Bernburg. As soon as the German pilots discovered this group flying alone, they attacked. Seven of the Three Hundred Sixth's Flying Fortresses were shot down and each of the remaining twenty-three aircraft were damaged, some seriously, during the constant German attacks while the group was on its bomb run and during the agonizing 200-mile return trip to the Channel. The bombing results of this unit were very good despite the attacks and the bad weather. Ju-88 production was cut to the extent of seventy to eighty percent temporarily.

Further to the west, a few bombers of the Three Hundred Eighty-Fourth that had become lost from their parent group joined the Three Hundred Third Group in a bomb run over the Aschersleben Motor works, where Ju-88s and other products for the Junkers complex were manufactured. There were thirty-four bombers in the attacking force and the bombardiers of this small American task force were so accurate that production was cut fifty percent at the plant for more than two months! The other heavy bombers of the First Division passed over their primary targets because of thick cloud cover and bombed targets of opportunity such at Arnhem, Deventer, Marburg, and Halberstadt, with varying and mostly insignificant results.

As a result, only ninety-nine heavy bombers of the Eighth Air Force task force dispatched from the English bases on the morning of February 22, 1944, succeeded in bombing the primary targets, and only 255 planes bombed any target at all! Their losses were much higher than on any previous Big Week mission—forty-one bombers failed to return to England that afternoon.

While the Eighth Air Force was having its difficulties in England and over the Continent on the third Big Week mission, the Fifteenth Air Force, flying out of the Foggia, Italy, airfield complex, was on its way to Regensburg. Twining's relatively new air force crews were unaware that because of the recall of the Third and Second Divisions of the Eighth Air Force and the trouble the First Division was having with the weather, they were flying directly into an aerial ambush set up by the Luftwaffe. Galland's fighter pilots had been alerted by German radar that an American air armada was heading north from Italy, and they were prepared. One of the obstacles faced by the Fifteenth Air Force that the Eighth Air Force did not face was the Alps. On the way to targets in Germany the B-17s and B-24s from Italy naturally had to climb to an altitude high enough to clear the mountains, and the German radar screens soon detected the American aircraft and passed the word to Galland's centralized fighter-control headquarters. In addition the turbulence encountered in the area of the mountains and the danger the peaks presented to a pilot whose plane had lost an engine or was damaged by enemy fighters or antiaircraft was grave.

"You can't ditch a Flying Fortress on a mountain peak," the Fifteenth Air Force pilots used to say in reference to the "easy" out the Eighth Air Force pilots had when in the same predicament—landing in the Channel.

The Fifteenth Air Force was not nearly as large as the Eighth Air Force. During February, 1944, the Fifth and Forty-Seventh Wings bore the brunt of the long strategic-bombing mission over the Alps to Germany in the Flying

Fortresses and Liberators. The Fifth Wing, commanded by Brigadier General Charles W. Wallace, who had taken over the leadership shortly before Big Week, had the Second, Ninety-Seventh, Ninety-Ninth, and Three Hundred First Groups available for missions. The Second Group had a long and distinguished history dating to its combat in France during the First World War. Between wars this unit had engaged in the Mitchell demonstrations of the effectiveness of aerial bombardment on battleships, flew mercy missions in the United States and other parts of the world, and made several good-will flights. In 1939, as the European conflict began to spread, the Second Group started training in B-17s. When the United States entered the war, the crews spent several months on antisubmarine duty and then went to North Africa to fly bombing missions. The group's personnel and equipment arrived at the airfield at Amendola, Italy, on December 9, 1943; and from that date on, the group flew both tactical missions in support of the ground troops in Italy and long-range strategic missions into Germany. Colonel Herbert E. Rice commanded the Second during Big Week.

The Ninety-Seventh Group had also seen a great deal of aerial combat action in England, North Africa, southern France, Sardinia, Sicily, and finally Italy. Colonel Frank Allen had brought the Ninety-Seventh to Italy in December, 1943, where it was first based at Cerignola and later Amendola. Another group that flew with the Ninety-Seventh quite often was the Ninety-Ninth Group, based at Tortorella Airfield and commanded by Colonel Ford J. Lauer, who had been appointed to the job seven days before the February 22, 1944, Big Week mission to Regensburg.

A fourth group of the Fifth Wing of the Fifteenth Air Force was the famed Three Hundred First Group, which had initially been a part of the Eighth Air Force and had

165

attacked submarine bases, airfields, railroads, bridges, and other targets on the Continent before moving to North Africa in November, 1942. Lieutenant Colonel Karl T. Barthelmess had taken command of the unit in December, 1943, when it arrived at Cerignola and just before the beginning of Big Week had moved the group to the airfield at Lucera, Italy. The Three Hundred First, like the Second, Ninety-Seventh, and Ninety-Ninth Groups, used B-17 aircraft.

The Forty-Seventh Wing, however, was a Liberator unit, and the competition between the B-17 and B-24 pilots was never-ending, with no decision ever being reached that satisfied all concerned. The Forty-Seventh had its headquarters at Manduria, Italy, in February, 1944, and was under the command of Brigadier General Joseph H. Atkinson, who assumed this responsibility on the eleventh of February, only nine days before the beginning of Big Week. This wing had the Ninety-Eighth, Three Hundred Seventy-Sixth, Four Hundred Forty-Ninth, Four Hundred Fiftieth, and Four Hundred Fifty-First on its roster. The Ninety-Eighth Group's claim to fame prior to Big Week was its mission to Ploesti on August 1, 1943, when Colonel John R. Kane, its group commander, received the Medal of Honor for leading the unit to the target despite the hazards of oil fires, delayed-action bombs, and alerted defenses. On February 22, 1944, the group was based at Lecce, Italy, and commanded by Lieutenant Colonel Marshall R. Gray.

Next door, at San Pancrazio, Italy, was Colonel Theodore Q. Graff's Three Hundred Seventy-Sixth Group, which had also been on the low-level raid to the Rumanian oil refineries at Ploesti in August, 1943, and was now ready to penetrate the Luftwaffe-defended Third Reich. The Four Hundred Forty-Ninth, Four Hundred Fiftieth, and Four Hundred Fifty-First were relatively new groups and had arrived in Italy directly from the United States during the weeks of December, 1943–January, 1944. The Four Hundred Forty-Ninth was commanded by Colonel Thomas J. Gent and was based at Grottaglie, Italy, after flying from Bruning AAF in Nebraska. The Four Hundred Fiftieth arrived at Manduria, Italy, from Alamogordo AAF, New Mexico, at about the same time and was commanded by Colonel John S. Mills. The Four Hundred Fifty-First flew to Algeria from Fairmont AAF, Nebraska, for a few weeks' extra training before Colonel Robert E. L. Eaton, the commander, brought the unit to Gioia del Colle, Italy, just before the beginning of Big Week.

Unfortunately the Three Hundred Fourth Wing of the Fifteenth Air Force, composed of the Four Hundred Fifty-Fourth, Four Hundred Fifty-Fifth, Four Hundred Fifty-Sixth, and Four Hundred Fifty-Ninth Groups, was just starting operations in the theater and was not at full strength in time for Big Week.

On February 22, 1944, the Fifth and Forty-Seventh Wings of the Fifteenth Air Force dispatched a force of 183 bombers against Regensburg, and 118 of the aircraft successfully bombed the Messerschmitt factory at Obertraubling. Serious damage resulted from the high explosives dropped by the Fifteenth Air Force, but the cost was high. Under constant and determined attack by a large number of twin-engine Ju-88s of Major General Huth's Number 7 Division in South Germany, Twining's Fifteenth Air Force lost fourteen heavy bombers.

It was a sad day for Doolittle's Eighth Air Force. Four hundred and ten men had been lost plus forty-one aircraft, and the primary German targets had not been damaged to the extent that the USAAF had planned. Fewer than one hundred bombers had attacked their main targets, and only slightly more than half the heavy bombers dispatched that morning from the English bases had bombed *any* target. At Park House in the suburbs of London, where Spaatz and his staff lived, there was gloom.

Big Week's third mission had undoubtedly been a big fiasco!

11
THE CRUCIAL MISSION

There was not the anticipated glee in Galland's head-quarters on the night of February 22, 1944, that Doolittle surmised. The Luftwaffe's commander of the fighter forces was delighted that his Ju-88s, Me-109s, and Fw-190s, with the help of other German fighter aircraft, had shot down a total of fifty-five Flying Fortresses and Liberators that day; but he was well aware that the cost had been high. The exact figure of fighter planes lost overall was still not available at dark, but he estimated that at least fifty Luftwaffe aircraft were missing in action. Galland knew he could not afford to lose so many planes, that he could not keep up the pace. The mounting fuel shortage, the serious damage to fighter planes, which were brought back to the Luftwaffe bases by the pilots, and the lack of replacement planes and fliers threatened to reduce the effectiveness of his forces seriously. The question that worried Galland on the night of February 22, 1944, was, would the weather over Germany remain clear enough for the American heavy bombers to continue their raids or would the clouds close in and give his fighter units a chance to recuperate?

"Check with Berlin about tomorrow's weather!" he ordered an aide.

Galland was getting a personal account of the day's action in the air from one of his division commanders when

169

the weather report arrived and was delivered to him. He took one look at the report and smiled.

"Heavy clouds are predicted," he said. "Good. That will give us time to rest and do some planning."

The planning that Galland had in mind was based on an all-out defensive effort to match the all-out offensive effort being launched by the Eighth Air Force. So far, during the week's three large American heavy-bomber missions deep into the Reich, he had directed what he considered an orthodox defense; but now, despite the German success of February 22, 1944, he was convinced the Luftwaffe had to do more, had to use every method, orthodox and unorthodox, to stop the USAAF bombers.

He realized, perhaps more than any other officer at the higher level of command in the German Air Force, just how critical the situation was becoming. If the Americans kept up the pressure, if the Flying Fortresses and Liberators kept flying into Germany in the same large numbers they had since the beginning of the week, the Luftwaffe was going to reach a point where its losses of men and equipment would not enable it to effectively oppose the American task forces. To Galland, as he prepared for the next major American raid on a German target, it was a now-or-never crisis!

Galland had more than his Me-262 rocket planes to use as secret weapons against the American heavy bombers. He had new tactics, new equipment, new theories. One new tactic was originated by several Luftwaffe fighter pilots who had been battling the Flying Fortresses for several months. Heinz Knoke was one of the German fliers who came to the conclusion that they could fly above the American bombers, which usually flew in close formation or combat boxes, and drop bombs on them!

The Me-109G was capable of carrying either four 100-pound bombs, a single 500-pound bomb, or a rack of antipersonnel bombs. He and several other pilots spent

170

long hours calculating velocities and trajectories, while ground personnel figured the fuse time that would be needed if the German pilots maintained a prescribed altitude above the bombers. It was finally decided that the Me-109s would fly approximately 3,000 feet above the Flying Fortresses or Liberators and drop 100-pound bombs with fifteen-second time fuses. After obtaining higher approval, Knoke and his flight crew spent several hours practicing the air-to-air bombing technique, using a tow target pulled by a Ju-88 as an aiming point.

Finally, Knoke went aloft in a Me-109 carrying a 500-pound bomb and dropped it on a B-17 formation. The bomb shattered the wing of one Flying Fortress, and the big bomber immediately spun to earth. After this initial success was reported to Galland, several Luftwaffe units were equipped to drop bombs on the American formations, but the new technique was only a partial success. However, on the night of February 22, 1944, Galland alerted these units to be prepared to use their bombing tactics against the Flying Fortresses and Liberators on the next mission.

Another call went out that night from Galland's headquarters to the storm-fighter units. These were elite units of fighters that were organized by Major von Kornatzki, based on the Japanese kamikaze tactics. Late in 1943 a suggestion was received from the front that volunteer German fighter pilots ram the American heavy bombers, especially the lead aircraft of each formation. Galland did not believe in such suicide attacks, so he and von Kornatzki devised the storm-fighter tactics instead. In place of ramming, the Luftwaffe fighters would attack the American formations while flying in tight formation themselves, closing as near as possible to the enemy bombers while firing.

The volunteer-manned storm-fighter units were equipped with FW-190s that carried four two-centimeter cannons and two three-centimeter MK-108 cannons. The cockpit was surrounded by heavy armor plate—to protect the pilot as he closed to within arm's reach of the Flying Fortresses and Liberators—as were other vital parts of the plane. The idea was very successful and Galland authorized a storm-fighter squadron for each wing of the Luftwaffe. These, too, were alerted by his headquarters on the night of February 22, 1944.

In addition Galland made certain that as many as possible of the Ju-88s—equipped with twenty-one-centimeter rockets, which could be fired from a distance of approximately 800 yards, the limit of the range of the effective fire from the Flying Fortresses and Liberators—were ready to oppose the next American heavy-bomber task force. These modified fighters had caused havoc among the close-flying American aircraft, since the German pilots could stay out of range of the machine guns aboard the bombers and lob the rockets in on the enemy planes.

Other German fighters—with bombs attached to long steel cables that were dragged through the American formations, the bombs exploding either on contact with a bomber or by an activating device in the cockpit of the German plane—were notified to be ready for an all-out effort. The German night fighters, especially the skilled pilots of the "Wild Boar" units, unequalled in daring and marksmanship in the Luftwaffe, were ordered to stand by for daytime defensive action. And even the secret "Mistel"—a unique combination of a Ju-88, heavily loaded with explosive charges, mounted on a Me-109 in such a manner that the pilot in the latter could release the Ju-88 at close range against a selected target—were ordered to full alert. The Mistel was designed for use against ships but Galland was desperate. He intended to do everything possible and use every weapon at his command to stop the next American heavy-bomber task force that tried to penetrate the skies over Germany—even to sending aloft some captured Flying Fortresses!

Doolittle at High Wycombe was feeling the pressure of Big Week, too, as he studied the weather reports for February 23, 1944. It appeared that the weather was going to be bad, that the Eighth Air Force would not be able to fly a mission. His feelings were mixed about the weather report from Krick. He knew that his forces needed a day to catch up on repairs on the planes that had battle damage and those that required mechanical adjustments on the engines. He was aware, too, that his crews were tired. Extremely tired. The reports from the flight surgeons were not encouraging. Many of the crewmen, officers and enlisted men, had been wounded; others had suffered frostbite and anoxia; and still others were showing signs of becoming "flak happy," a term used by the airmen to denote battle fatigue. The long raids, three days in a row for many of the fliers, were taking their toll. Perhaps a day's rest would help these men.

Yet, on the other hand, Doolittle realized the value of maintaining a constant pressure on the German defenses. If *his* pilots were tired, he knew that Galland's fighter pilots were also weary. He didn't want to give the Luftwaffe fliers time to recuperate or their ground personnel time to repair the Me-109s and FW-190s that had been so effective on the third mission.

The weather on February 23, 1944, resolved the dilemma for Doolittle, however. There was no possibility of launching a mission from the English bases since the overcast had closed all the airfields. Twining managed to dispatch 102 heavy bombers from Italy, and these Fifteenth Air Force planes destroyed twenty percent of Steyr Walzlagerwerke ball-bearing plant in Austria. That was it for the twenty-third.

The morning of February 24, 1944, however, was ideal for another trip into Germany, and Doolittle took advantage of it to launch a full-scale coordinated mission. He decided to make a maximum effort against Schweinfurt's ball-bearing plants, undoubtedly the most important in the Axis domain. He scheduled five combat wings of the First Division to bomb Schweinfurt, knowing that this target would be defended by Galland's fliers to the last German fighter plane. In addition, he dispatched three combat wings of the Second Division to attack the Gothaer Waggonfabrik A.G. at Gotha, Hitler's largest producer of twin-engine Me-110s, and five combat wings of the Third Division to bomb aircraft plants and assembly areas in northeastern Germany and at Tutow, Kreising, and Posen in Poland, all of which produced the deadly FW-190. Rostock was given as the alternate target. Altogether 867 bombers of the Eighth Air Force were dispatched on February 24, 1944, in the three task forces. In addition the Fifteenth Air Force in Italy sent 114 heavy bombers back to Steyr to bomb the Daimler-Puch aircraft plant.

Doolittle's overall plan for this mission on the fifth day of Big Week was carefully thought out and, for the most part, succeeded in its aim. The five combat wings of the Third Division that were again sent along the northern route to targets in northeastern Germany and Poland were covering a distance that was too great even for escort by the long-range American fighter planes.

It was another of Doolittle's calculated risks. He surmised that if he dispatched the Second and First Divisions earlier toward their targets in central Germany, the German radar observers would concentrate on these two task forces and would not send many Luftwaffe fighters north, away from this main body of enemy bombers, to intercept the smaller task force heading for the Tutow-Kreising-Posen area.

Not all his aides at High Wycombe agreed with Doolittle, some predicting an aerial massacre of the Third Division if he persisted in sending its aircraft that far without fighter escort; but the general refused to change the field order. Fortunately his analysis of the situation proved correct even though he did have a helping hand from the weather. The Third Division, flying through an overcast part of the trip, met very little fighter opposition but had to bomb Rostock, the secondary target, by H2X because of the weather.

The Second Division, however, despite having fighter escort, met Galland's pilots shortly after crossing the enemy coast and had their company all the way to and back from the target at Gotha. The 239 B-24s, consisting of eight groups of twenty-five to thirty bombers each, had left England ahead of the B-17s of the First Division in the belief that their unusually large formations would provide adequate defense against any Luftwaffe attacks as long as they also had fighter escort to keep the German fighters occupied part of the time. The officers and men of the Second Division hadn't considered the fact that Galland still had some secret techniques to use against them and that the German commander of the fighters intended to use them all on February 24, 1944.

Shortly after crossing the Dutch coast, Lieutenant Roger Bates of the Second Division saw three Ju-88s high above his formation. He watched the trio of German planes closely as they closed the horizontal distance between themselves and the B-24s, aware that the German pilots might be planning to drop bombs on the formation of heavy bombers, although American intelligence officers had briefed the crews that the bombs were usually dropped by Me-109s. Since the Ju-88s were out of range of the machine guns aboard his Liberator, there was nothing Bates could do but watch the twin-engine German planes as they passed overhead. After the Ju-88s disappeared from his view through the cockpit window, he alerted the tail gunner to watch the three enemy planes. For a few minutes there was no report from the tail section, but suddenly the gunner in the rear compartment called a warning over the interphone.

175

"The Ju-88s are making a one hundred eighty-degree turn and are following our formation," he said. "They are still over eight hundred feet above us."

"Roger. Watch them."

Again there was silence for several minutes until the tail gunner reported again. This time his voice was high-pitched, tense. "I can't figure it out but the Number Six plane in our formation just blew up. No flak in the area but the plane just exploded. . . . My god, there goes another one. . . . Number Five just exploded!"

"Where are the Ju-88s?" Bates asked quickly.

"Right above us but gaining fast. Do you . . . ? Hey, I see something hanging from a cable attached to one of the Ju-88s."

That was enough for Bates. Ordering the tail gunner to keep him posted on the position of the "something hanging from a cable," the lieutenant called down two Mustangs on the Ju-88s. By carefully maneuvering his B-24, Bates managed to evade the bomb on the cable until the pair of P-51s arrived. The Mustang pilots quickly shot down one of the Ju-88s while the other two German planes turned and dove headlong for the deck in an effort to escape. Two B-24s with the entire crews of both planes were lost, however. It was evident that Galland's secret weapons were taking their toll.

The Second Wing of the Second Division was in the lead as the B-14s headed for Gotha, but owing to a different wind velocity and direction than had been forecast for the route, this wing was far ahead of schedule and flying by itself as it neared the target area. The fighter aircraft of the Luftwaffe Number One Division, seeing this box all alone, concentrated on it with every available fighter plane. All the way to the aircraft plant at Gotha, the Me-109s and FW-190s made pass after pass through the Second Wing formations in a desperate effort to break up the attack.

As the B-24s turned on the target run from the initial point, the lead plane of the Three Hundred Eighty-Ninth Group of the Second Wing had a failure of its oxygen system. The pilot, suffering from the lack of the vital oxygen, lost control of the B-24 and veered off course. The bombardier passed out from the same cause and collapsed over the bombsight, accidently tripping the release and sending the bombs astray. The remainder of the Three Hundred Eighty-Ninth Group also bombed, but fortunately the other group of the Second Wing recognized the error and bombed the primary target as planned.

The Four Hundred Forty-Fifth Group of the Second Wing had to detour around the wandering Three Hundred Eighty-Ninth Group and bomb the target alone and consequently was by itself as it headed back toward England. The German fighters then centered their attention on this group and shot down thirteen of its total of twenty-five B-24s. Nine others were seriously damaged by the persistent Luftwaffe fighter attacks. Meanwhile the Three Hundred Eighty-Ninth Group was trying to get back on the proper course with the other formations; but while it was alone, the German pilots closed in and shot down six of its B-24s!

The Fourteenth Wing of the Second Division was jumped by the fighter planes of the Luftwaffe Number 3 Division as soon as they crossed the Dutch coast on the way to Gotha. Included in these attacks was one by a Mistel on the planes of the Three Hundred Ninety-Second Group.

Lieutenant Harold Martin, a replacement pilot who had joined the group just before Big Week, thought he was imagining things when he saw what appeared to be a Ju-88 "sitting" on a Me-109. He wasn't, as he soon discovered. The Ju-88, loaded with high explosives, was released at a precise moment by the German pilot in the mother Me-109 and flew directly toward the Three Hundred

177

Ninety-Second Group's formation. Martin, thinking it was a manned enemy fighter, waited for the German pilot in the twin-engine fighter to start firing his cannon or launch his rockets. To his horror the Ju-88 continued on course directly into the formation of close-flying Liberators and crashed into a plane flying in the low squadron. Both the Ju-88 and the B-24 exploded in midair. A few minutes later the lieutenant saw three other Mistels at a distance, but before the German pilots could release their lethal Ju-88s, the Mustang-escorting pilots chased them away. It wasn't until he returned to England that afternoon that Martin learned what type of secret weapon he had encountered. Even then it was difficult to believe.

Fortunately the Three Hundred Ninety-Second Group, including Martin, did not allow the Luftwaffe fighter attacks to deter them from their mission of bombing the aircraft plant at Gotha. This group dropped nearly a hundred percent of their bombs within 2,000 feet of the aiming point, while the other group of the Fourteenth Wing, the Forty-Fourth, did just about as well. Almost every building in the factory area was damaged; and the eastern half of the plant, where most of the aircraft production facilities were centered, was destroyed. The cost was high, however. The Three Hundred Ninety-Second Group lost seven B-24s during the mission, and thirteen of the remaining planes were extensively damaged by enemy fire.

While the Second Division Liberators were battling their way to Gotha through the throng of German fighters waiting for them, the First Division Flying Fortresses were having their troubles as they tried to reach Schweinfurt. And the trouble started early, in an unexpected manner ... the arrival of a renegade B-17! Most of American heavy-bomber crews involved with Big Week were unaware that the Luftwaffe was using captured Flying Fortresses in a variety of ways. Initially most of the captured B-17s that were airworthy were assigned to the "Rosarius

178

Flying Circus," a Luftwaffe unit composed of all operating captured planes, which traveled throughout Germany and the occupied countries to familiarize Luftwaffe pilots with the aircraft and their capabilities. Later a German Air Force group, the notorious I/K G200, was formed. This unit used captured Flying Fortresses for ferrying, parachuting, and supplying secret agents by air, especially in long-range operations.

These uses of the captured bombers, while having a certain nuisance value, didn't materially affect the operations of the Eighth Air Force. Later, however, Luftwaffe officers decided to use the renegade B-17s to detect American heavy-bomber task forces enroute to Germany and to supply a continous report on the course, speed and altitude of the formation to fighter-control headquarters. These eyewitness reports were more accurate than radar reports and were of great value. At other times the German crews in captured B-17s would infiltrate a formation and covertly shoot down one or more B-17s manned by American crews without the other crews in the group realizing what was going on.

Captain Detrick Stern of the First Division had listened to a British officer detail the exploits of I/K G200 early in February while he was in London, never thinking he would personally encounter one of the German-manned B-17s. As his formation passed Enschede in the Netherlands on the morning of February 24, 1944, Stern spotted a suspicious dot on the horizon to his left.

"Bogie, nine o'clock level," he warned his crew. "Keep an eye on him."

The captain was busy flying the big bomber and keeping it in the proper position in the formation, but every few seconds he glanced towards the speck on the horizon. Three thousand feet above his First Division formation he could see the P-47 and P-51 escort planes circling lazily. Apparently they had not spotted the lone plane closing from the north. The black dot was larger now and materializing into wings and a tail, but it was still too far away for Stern to determine what type of aircraft it was.

"It's just another Fortress," his left waist gunner reported suddenly over the interphone. "It must be lost from its own formation and is joining ours."

Stern heard his gunners laughing and knew that they were swinging their guns away from the newcomer now that they knew it was another B-17. For a few minutes he forgot about the stranger, too, but he suddenly recalled the discussion he had had in London with the Britisher about the German-manned B-17s and he decided, for safety's sake, to have another look at the newcomer. He made a slight correction in his heading and stared at the intruder. It was flying parallel to the formation at the same altitude as though the pilot were trying to use the guns of the First Division group to help protect his own aircraft. There was no group, squadron, or division insignia painted on the fuselage or tail as was usual with Eighth Air Force aircraft; but Stern knew that because of the unusual demand for new planes to fly missions during Big Week, time was not always taken to paint the insignia on newly arrived aircraft.

He was still studying the other B-17 when his navigator reported that the formation was approaching the IP where a sharp right turn was required. Once the IP was reached the strange Flying Fortress would have to be ignored just as enemy fighters and antiaircraft had to be as preference was given to bombing the target the B-17s had come so far to attack. Stern concentrated on holding the correct course as he approached the IP so he could make as perfect a bomb run as possible, but just before it was time to make the right turn a German antiaircraft shell exploded underneath the left wing of his Flying Fortress.

"The number three engine has stopped. Oil pouring from it," the waist gunner reported.

Stern had no choice but to feather the damaged engine and drop out of the formation so that he would not interfere with the bomb run the other planes of the group were starting at the time. Very slowly he eased the control wheel to the left and started a shallow descending turn. He was partially through the maneuver before he was aware that he was turning directly toward the strange Flying Fortress. As he closed the gap between his aircraft and the newcomer, he was surprised to see the other B-17 bank sharply away.

"Bogies. Twelve o'clock level!" a gunner reported.

Stern glanced toward the designated area and saw a swarm of enemy fighters heading directly toward the formation, which was now on its bomb run and very vulnerable. He suspected then that he had been correct: The B-17 was a renegade manned by Germans that had guided the Luftwaffe fighters to the scene. He also knew that the renegade crew would call down several of the German fighters to attack him and his crew since they were alone and flying on only three engines. He didn't have long to wait to verify this prediction.

"Four FW-190s approaching at nine o'clock high," his top turret gunner called.

"Roger. Watch them and also keep an eye on the gunners in that other B-17. I think that is a German crew!"

The captain didn't have time to explain further. Knowing that his single plane couldn't withstand the onslaught of so many enemy fighters, Stern made a quick decision. He eased his B-17 in as close as possible to the German-manned B-17 before the startled Luftwaffe pilot was aware of what was happening. Overlapping his wingtip with the other plane's wingtip, the captain hoped that the German fighters would hesitate to fire for fear of hitting their own comrades in the captured Flying Fortress.

"You're going to hit him," the waist gunner in Stern's plane cried as the captain slid in closer.

181

Even as the waist gunner's voice came over the interphone, the captain saw the FW-190s start their first pass. Watching them closely, he ruddered his plane so close to the German-manned B-17 that his left wingtip threatened to go into the other aircraft's waist window. The enemy fighters, however, didn't alter course. They kept diving straight for the two B-17s, and it appeared they were willing to sacrifice the German bomber crew in order to down the American bomber crew. Stern waited for the cannon in the wings of the FW-190s to start flashing as the German pilots began firing but the flashes never came. Instead, the FW-190s roared past and began a slow turn to the right. Not a shot had been fired!

Before Stern and his crew had a chance to congratulate themselves on their good fortune, the sound of machine-gun fire echoed even above the noise of the bomber's engines, and his B-17 shuddered. The Germans in the other Flying Fortress had opened fire on his bomber!

"Number one engine is losing oil," the top turret gunner called. "The whole wing is black with it."

Stern stared at his instruments. The oil-temperature needle was in the red, the supply needle was at zero. The oil cooler had been hit.

"Feathering number one!"

With only two engines running, the captain still managed to stay with the renegade Flying Fortress because of his much greater experience in flying the bomber. Everytime the German-manned B-17 turned, Stern turned with it, knowing his survival depended upon sticking close to the German. Banking right, left, diving—the two bombers remained within a few feet of each other, the gunners firing steadily across the narrow gap.

Meanwhile Stern had his radio operator trying to contact the American fighters overhead on the radio set in the radio compartment, while the copilot was calling the Mustangs on the VHF set. For several minutes there was

182

no reply from the escorting fighters, since they were busily engaged in keeping the main group of Luftwaffe fighters from the formations of Flying Fortresses that had dropped their bombs and were now heading back toward the Channel.

Finally the copilot contacted two P-51s, and the Mustangs came down to help. Stern identified his own B-17 by firing a red flare, and the Mustangs—after a short engagement with the FW-190s, during which one German fighter was shot down and one damaged—attacked the renegade Flying Fortress. Other P-51s joined the battle, and despite repeated attempts by as many as ten Luftwaffe fighter planes to protect the German-manned B-17, the captured bomber was shot down.

Stern managed to fly his damaged Flying Fortress back to England on the two remaining engines after dropping his bombs on a target of opportunity on the German border. The facts he gave to American intelligence concerning the tactics of the captured B-17 flown by the German crew were valuable and were used to brief American bomber crews as they prepared for future missions.

The damage inflicted on the Schweinfurt ball-bearing plants by the heavy bombers of the First Divison of February 24, 1944, was considerable but not as much as had been caused by the costly raid of October 14, 1943. The 238 B-17s dropped 574.3 tons of high explosives and incendiaries on the target area on the twenty-fourth, resulting in major damage to three of the four ball-bearing plants. Direct hits were achieved on machine shops, storage buildings, and power stations. One First Division formation, unable to see the target visually because of heavy smoke over the area, dropped its high explosives on a jelly factory and a malt works! Altogether the First Division lost eleven heavy bombers, while their gunners claimed 108 Luftwaffe fighters, a reflection of the intensity of the aerial battle.

The Fifteenth Air Force bombers out of Italy experienced difficulties from the beginning of the mission on February 24, 1944, until it was over that night. Originally Twining sent 114 aircraft to bomb the Daimler-Puch aircraft-component plant at Steyr, but by the time the formations crossed the Alps on the way north, twenty-seven of the heavy bombers had become separated from the main force. These twenty-seven planes finally dropped their high explosives on the Fiume oil refinery, while the remaining eighty-seven B-17s continued on to Steyr, where they bombed the primary target.

During the trip into the target and back out, the main force of the Fifteenth Air Force experienced every Galland trick in his repetoire: Coordinated attacks by four to six single-engine fighters, Ju-88s firing rockets from long range, Me-109s dropping bombs on the formation, and even two Mistel attacks harassed the B-17s from Italy. Seventeen of the heavy bombers of the task force were shot down, ten from one formation! The damage to the target was minimal owing to the persistent and determined Luftwaffe fighter attacks during the bomb run.

The cost of the February 24, 1944, mission was high, with the Second Division losing a total of thirty-three heavy bombers; the First Division, eleven aircraft; and the Fifteenth Air Force, seventeen planes. Only the Third Division, which went north to Rostock without fighter escort, escaped unscathed. In addition ten American fighters were shot down during dogfights that cost the Luftwaffe thirty-seven aircraft.

Spirits were good at High Wycombe, however, despite the tragic loss of men and planes because after the debriefing reports had been studied, the reconnaissance photographs developed and analyzed, and the intelligence summary reviewed, Doolittle was aware that Galland had used every resource at his command to stop the American bombers—and had failed. He noted that the German

184

commander of the fighters had used his secret weapons, his night fighters, his rocket planes (which had not been very successful on the twenty-fourth because of the route taken by the heavy bombers), and had even personally directed some of the Luftwaffe units in their desperate bid to turn the B-17s and B-24s back from the targets the American crew men had been ordered to attack. It had undoubtedly been the most intense aerial battle of Big Week, but there was no denying the results. The Flying Fortresses and Liberators had taken everything Galland could throw in their path and had continued to the assigned targets, dropped their bombs with commendable accuracy, and had returned to their bases with losses that, while high, were still considerably lower than had been predicted before the launching of Big Week. There was no doubt in Doolittle's mind that his Eighth Air Force had shown the Luftwaffe on February 24, 1944, that it could go where it wanted, bomb whatever target it desired, and do it whenever is wished to do so.

Other American and British officers, some of much higher rank, were not so certain, however. Seeing was believing. They wanted to see the daring general's Eighth Air Force do it again.

12
THE CLIMAX

The stage was set for the climax blow, which fell on the
sixth day of Big Week. Even weatherman Krick cooper-
ated and announced that the weather on February 25,
1944, would be so clear over the Continent that Doolittle
could select any target in Germany he wanted to attack
and feel confident that his bombardiers could drop their
high explosives visually. Some military men thought that
Doolittle might rest on his laurels and select an easy mission for the twenty-fifth. Now could they blame him if he
did. After five days of concentrated and dangerous action
his crews deserved a milk run, if any target in Germany
could be so classified.

The general, however, had no desire for further plaudits
for himself or his Eighth Air Force. He was interested in
only one thing—achieving air superiority over the Continent so that the cross-Channel invasion could be launched
as planned. With this in mind, he and the USSTAF
planners drew some red lines across the map of Europe
that caused veteran officers at High Wycombe to shudder
when they looked at them. It was obvious that Doolittle
wasn't going to take any halfway measures in his effort
to show Galland who controlled the skies over Europe.

He decided to launch a full-scale attack against the remaining high-priority objectives in southern Germany—
both Messerschmitt factories at Regensburg, the Messerschmitt parent plant at Augsburg, the V.F.K. bearing

plant at Stuttgart and the Bachmann-Von Blumenthal factory at Furth, which manufactured components for the Me-110. The Fifteenth Air Force aircraft from Italy were assigned the Messerschmitt component plant at Regensburg-Prufening. Approximately 1,300 American bombers took to the air over England and Italy on the morning of February 25, 1944, one of the largest US aerial task forces ever to launch an attack against targets in one area.

A total of 1,000 fighters were assigned escorting duties for this massive heavy-bomber armada.

When such a large number of men are involved in an operation, whether it is on the ground or in the air, unusual events are certain to occur. The stress of a week of steady combat had resulted in many of the bomber-crew men reaching that delicate borderline between normalcy and abnormalcy—a border line that was often undetected by flight surgeons and group commanders. The mission of February 25, 1944, the last operation of Big Week, harbored at least two mysteries that were never revealed in official documents but were well known to those airmen and officers who survived the ordeal. One of the mysteries answered that day dealt with the "Mad Gunner of the Fortresses".

A flight surgeon of the One Hundredth Group of the Third Division had first notified High Wycombe about the mad gunner when a dead crew man, brought home in a bomber after the bombing of Brunswick on February 21, 1944, was discovered to have died from a fifty-caliber shell. At first it was thought to have been accidental. During the confusion and tenseness of an air battle, when one group of bombers flew almost within arm's reach of another group and both groups being penetrated by Luftwaffe fighters, it was entirely possible that some fifty-caliber rounds could go wild. When several other airmen died from fifty-caliber shells within the next three days, however, it became evident that there was more than an accidental firing involved. When a bombardier of a Third Division group was killed by the gun of another B-17 while the formation was crossing the target area on February 24, 1944, and there were no antiaircraft or enemy fighters within miles, there was no longer any doubt that a mad gunner was on the loose among the crew men.

At a meeting of division flight surgeons it was agreed that the mad gunner was probably a crew man who had been unable to withstand the mental stress of so many long-range missions and had gone berserk. It was also agreed there was a possibility that this man was not even aware of what he was doing, that during the intensity of battle he was temporarily insane. Each pilot in the division was ordered to assemble his crew on the night of the twenty-fourth and explain the situation to them and warn them to be on the alert for such a crew member. Naturally each pilot denied that the mad gunner was on his crew.

One of the pilots who denied the possibility of his Flying Fortress harboring such a man—a veteran flier of the Ninety-Fifth Group of the Third Division who testified later at a division staff meeting—was shocked when he heard a gun on his B-17 open fire as the plane crossed the enemy coastline on February 25, 1944. When he couldn't see any enemy fighters approaching from the left side of the heavy bomber, he asked the copilot if there were any Luftwaffe fighters in view on the right side. The answer was negative.

"Who's firing back there?" the pilot asked.

A waist gunner reported that it was the ball-turret gunner, a crew man who ranked as one of the most courageous men the pilot had ever known. The ball turret was a dangerous and vulnerable three-foot diameter glass ball hanging from the belly of the Flying Fortress and few airmen volunteered to ride in it. This man, a West Virginia coal miner before the war, never complained and stayed in the glass ball from just after takeoff to just before landing, protecting the underside of the aircraft from Luftwaffe fighters.

"Ball turret, what are you firing at?" the perplexed pilot asked.

There was no immediate answer. Instead, the guns in the ball turret continued to fire for several seconds. Finally the tense voice of the ball-turret gunner came over the interphone.

"They're coming after us. Can't you see them? See, there's one now!"

A quick check by the pilot revealed that another B-17 was moving into the wing position on the left to fill an empty slot and the mad gunner in the ball turret was firing toward it. The pilot—knowing there was a distinct possibility of his ball-turret gunner killing someone in the other bomber or perhaps, in his mental condition, even shooting it down—quickly pulled his plane out of the formation and drifted about a mile to the left of the group. He maintained his altitude, however, since he wanted to rejoin the formation as soon as he got the crazed ball-turret gunner out of the glass ball. A lone B-17 over enemy territory was nearly always a sure statistic for a Luftwaffe fighter pilot. When the other crew members tried to get the mad gunner out of the ball turret, however, they soon discovered they had a problem. The gunner kept the turret revolving electrically so fast that they could not stop it in the stowed position. The bewildered pilot considered cutting the electrical power long enough to crank the ball turret into the stowed position by hand and get the beserk gunner out. But he decided it was too risky; too much of the equipment in the plane was operated by electrical power, and to shut it off, even temporarily, might cause disaster.

While he was still trying to discover a way to get the gunner out of the ball turret, his B-17 was attacked by four FW-190s, and two engines were damaged so severely they had to be feathered. On the second pass the Luftwaffe fighters made at the lone Flying Fortress, part of the control cables were severed and the life raft over the radio compartment was jarred loose and caught in the vertical tail section of the bomber, jamming the rudder.

The pilot had a difficult time holding the plane level, even with the control wheel turned all the way to the left and using maximum trim. Knowing it was only a matter of time before he would loose complete control of the aircraft, he ordered the crew to bail out. Unfortunately, as the gunners prepared to jump, two of the FW-190s roared in for another attack and it was impossible for them to bail out unless they wanted to risk being struck by the fire from the enemy fighters.

At that moment the ball-turret gunner, firing at any plane, American or German, that approached the B-17 in which he was riding, swung his guns toward the two FW-190s. He shot the canopy off the lead fighter and evidently wounded the pilot, because according to the testimony of the surviving crew members, the first FW-190 swerved sharply and collided with the second Luftwaffe plane. They both burst into flames and spun to earth.

This gave the crew men aboard the doomed Flying Fortress the time they needed and they all bailed out except the pilot, who struggled to hold the plane straight and level a few minutes longer. After he was certain his crew had jumped, the pilot checked his own parachute pack and prepared to release the controls and try to get out through the nose hatch before the B-17 went into a spin and trapped him. Just before he released the controls, however, he called the ball-turret gunner once more on the interphone.

"Ball turret, do you hear me?"

There was no answer and the pilot, knowing he had very little time left to get out of the burning aircraft, turned to head for the nose hatch. At that moment, a pitiful call reached his ears through the earphones still on his head.

"My god, what did I do?"

The pilot recognized the voice of the ball-turret gunner immediately and asked him if he was all right.

"I guess so, but when I came to my senses a while ago I was shooting at another B-17. I didn't hit it, did I?"

The pilot tried to convince him that everything was all right, that the important thing now was to bail out immediately, but the ball-turret gunner, realizing that he probably had shot at other planes in the formation on earlier raids, that he was the "mad" gunner everyone was searching for, refused to jump.

The desperate pilot stayed with the doomed B-17 as long as he could, but when it finally did a wingover and started into a spin, he bailed out. He was rescued from the Channel four hours later. The remainder of his crew, which had bailed out earlier, were captured by the Germans and taken prisoner. Only the ball-turret gunner died, and the fact that he was the so-called mad gunner was never revealed except at a private meeting at High Wycombe a week later. It was decided that he had given his most treasured possession—his life—in return for the hope that he would be forgiven. He was.

The Eighth Air Force task force was able to bomb the primary targets on February 25, 1944, with good-to-excellent accuracy. Even though the crews were tired, "flak happy," as evidenced by the extreme case of the ball-turret gunner, and apprehensive, the First, Second, and Third Divisions did considerable damage to the aircraft plants, especially at Regensburg and Augsburg. Regensburg was the center of the Me-109 production, and Doolittle hoped that his heavy bombers on the twenty-fifth could finish the job that had been started months before and had cost so many American lives. The Fifteenth Air Force had tried to complete the job on February 22,

1944, but with the odds against its task force, many of the production facilities were still standing as the final mission of Big Week began. The Eighth Air Force bombed both factories at Regensburg on the twenty-fifth, and when the attack was completed none of the buildings had escaped undamaged. Many were totally destroyed. Plant records obtained from German sources later indicated that production fell from 435 planes per month in January, 1944, to 135 per month in March, 1944, as a direct result of the bombing. It took the Regensburg complex four months to reach its production schedule again after the February 25, 1944, attack by the Third Division heavy bombers.

The First Division did similar damage to the Messerschmitt plant at Augsburg, where its high-explosive bombs destroyed thirty buildings and reduced production by thirty-five percent. Nearly half of the valuable, irreplaceable machine tools were damaged; and three-fourths of all material stored at the Augsburg plant was completely ruined. While less damage was done to the plant and finished aircraft at Furth by the Second Division, it was obvious that Hitler's production facilities had suffered a severe setback, one that would have a direct bearing on the forthcoming cross-Channel invasion by the Allies.

The Eighth Air Force once again proved—just as Doolittle had predicted twenty-four hours earlier after the February 24, 1944, mission—that it was now the superior air force over the Continent. The Luftwaffe managed to shoot down only thirty-one heavy bombers of the massive aerial armada that went to Germany on this last mission of Big Week, while the Americans bombed their primary targets at will. With the proper fighter escort by long-range P-51s over the target area and protection by the P-38s and P-47s on the penetration and withdrawal, the strategic bombers of the USAAF ruled the sky over Hitler's Germany as well as the countries his troops had occupied.

Unfortunately the Fifteenth Air Force from Italy

lacked escort of sufficiently long range to provide protection during the most distant phase of its mission to Regensburg, and the Luftwaffe took advantage of this fact. Furthermore, since only its bombers equipped for long missions could reach the target area, the remainder of the task force from Italy had to bomb shorter-range targets, such as rail yards and port installations at Fiume, the harbor area at Zara, warehouses at Pola, rail lines at Zell-am-See, and the runways at the airfield near Graz-Thalerhof. Only 176 of the Fifteenth Air Force bombers went to Regensburg, while the remainder of the 400-plane task force bombed the much closer targets.

Major General Huth, the German commander of Luftwaffe Number 7 Division, watched the reports of the approaching bombers in his operations bunker at Schleissheim, near Munich, on February 25, 1944, and was faced with a decision. One task force of heavy bombers, the Third Division, was approaching Regensburg from the west, while a second task force, the Fifteenth Air Force, was approaching the same area from the south. He finally decided to pit the bulk of his fighters against the southern task force because as yet no American fighter escort had been detected. It was an opportune decision for the German commander and his Luftwaffe planes shot down thirty-three American heavy bombers, nearly one-fifth of the Fifteenth Air Force task force! The only consolation as far as the USAAF was concerned was that while the Luftwaffe concentrated on the American bombers from Italy, the bombers from England destroyed the target.

Once again the air crews faced an overwhelming enemy fighter force, as the harried Fifteenth Air Force bombers desperately tried to reach Regensburg on the twenty-fifth, and the strain on the men began to show in various ways. Aerial combat in World War II, especially during the long, daily missions of Big Week, subjected airmen to emotional stresses mankind had never known before. While these stresses were no more severe than those experienced by men engaged in ground warfare, they were new and it was difficult for even trained medical men to know the exact hour when ordinary fatigue deteriorated into mental breakdown. The feeling of naked vulnerability to antiaircraft and enemy fighters that most airmen felt as they crouched in their bombers miles above the ground led to many strange episodes in the air. Sometimes it was just a minor mental quirk. At other times it could lead to tragedy or near-tragedy. One such near-tragedy occurred during the Fifteenth Air Force's mission to Regensburg on February 25, 1944. The following report by a new copilot on a Fifteenth Air Force B-24 gives a detailed account of the incident.

It was my first combat mission and I was flying copilot for Lieutenant ———, a veteran of several months of combat with both the Eighth and Fifteenth Air Forces. During takeoff, formation assembly, and the flight across the Alps, this pilot had handled the bomber very well. Even when the high squadron leader had been forced to abort the mission because of engine trouble, the lieutenant had moved into the lead slot without a moment's hesitation. As we neared Regensburg and the flak and fighters threatened our formation, however, I noticed a distinct change in the pilot. He stared straight ahead and wouldn't answer me when I spoke to him over the interphone. Since this was my first mission and I was new with the group, I was unaware that the lieutenant had just returned to combat at the beginning of the month after a rest and medical treatment for a nervous condition. Consequently I was not prepared for his next action.

194

As two Me-109s attacked our aircraft, the lieutenant suddenly banked our bomber out of the formation . . . or tried to do so. The other pilots of the high squadron were confused by his action but they did as they had been trained to do—they followed him. The entire squadron separated from the main group formation. While I was still trying to determine why the lieutenant had turned away from the other aircraft, I heard the gear extending into the airstream and discovered that the lieutenant was holding the switch in the down position. Before I could stop him he also lowered half-flaps and began screaming for the crew to bail out over the interphone.

When the German fighters came at us again, the lieutenant again picked up the microphone and ordered the crew not to shoot, explaining that if they didn't shoot at the Luftwaffe pilots, they would be permitted to bail out without being shot by the German fliers. Since our aircraft had not been damaged, we had no wounded crew men aboard, and there was no apparent reason why we should bail out. I decided that something was radically wrong with the lieutenant.

The copilot, a second lieutenant, explained that after one look at the German countryside four miles below he made up his mind that he was not bailing out as long as the B-24 would still fly. During those first confused minutes the top-turret gunner left his position long enough to go to the cockpit to warn the copilot about the lieutenant.

The top-turret gunner tapped me on the shoulder and yelled for me to take over the controls, that the lieutenant had gone beserk *again*. That word *again* stuck in my mind as I grabbed the control wheel and I wondered what the top-turret gunner meant. I soon discovered that I couldn't budge the controls. The lieutenant had a death grip on the wheel and I couldn't even force his fingers loose a fraction of an inch. Seeing my difficulty, the top-turret gunner grabbed the lieutenant around the neck from his position back of the pilot seat and began choking him. The lieutenant, however, was completely beserk and with one swing of his right arm he slammed the top-turret gunner's head against a fire extinguisher and the crewman's walk-around oxygen bottle disengaged from his mask. The lack of oxygen and the blow on the head was too much for the top-turret gunner and he passed out. Fortunately, while the lieutenant was dealing with the top-turret gunner, I managed to wrench the control wheel from his grip. I immediately eased our plane underneath main formation for added protection from the attacking German fighters only to discover that the group was now on the bomb run and had their bomb-bay doors open. Knowing that we were doomed if the bombs dropped on our B-24, I slid out to the right of the other aircraft and hoped for the best.

It took more than hope! The lieutenant grabbed the wheel again in a desperate attempt to regain control of the plane but the copilot made a quick move. Seeing that the lieutenant had unloosened his safety belt in preparation for bailing out, the copilot pushed the control wheel forward as hard as he could and when the nose of the plane dropped sharply, the lieutenant flew out of his seat. His head hit hard against the top of the cockpit, and while he was dazed a waist gunner, who had come forward to the cockpit to help, pulled the lieutenant out of the seat, sat him on the floor of the cockpit, and strapped his hands together with a parachute harness. The waist gunner also put another walk-around bottle on the top turret gunner and revived him.

While this was going on, I tried to lead the high squadron back into the proper position in the formation. I realized that our only chance was to regroup. Before I could get back with the other planes, our number three engine was hit by cannon fire from a FW-190 and set afire, but we managed to get the flames under control within a few minutes. Finally we regrouped and the Luftwaffe fighters in the area decided to leave us alone and attack the formation behind us which, for some reason, was now scattered all over the sky. We had a relatively uneventful trip back to base despite the feathered engine; but as I prepared to land, the lieutenant managed to break loose from the parachute harness that the waist gunner had used to tie his hands. He seized the control wheel unexpectedly while I was on the approach and at low altitude, screaming again that we should all bail out, but with the help of the gunners I maintained control of the aircraft and made a successful landing. The medics then took over.

The berserk lieutenant was hospitalized and at once taken permanently off flight status. After his case—and the cases of several other pilots who had been returned to combat after treatment for nervous breakdowns caused by previous combat missions—was studied it was decided that the risk was too great to try to rehabilitate the majority of such fliers. Evidence indicated that a large percentage of the pilots that were considered "cured" could not withstand the stress of combat a second time and often endangered the lives of their crews and the crews of other aircraft in the formation.

After the mission of February 25, 1944, a low-pressure system moved over western and central Europe and the weather turned bad. Big Week was over!

HOW BIG WAS BIG WEEK?

The results of Big Week have long been discussed and argued by those who took part in the operation, historians who didn't, German military experts, Albert Speer (whose ministry took over Germany's aircraft production), USAAF officers, and many others who have studied the series of American heavy-bomber missions of February, 1944. It is fairly easy for all of these individuals to agree on some facts and figures, impossible for them to agree on others. It is a known fact that more than 3,300 heavy bombers from the Eighth Air Force and more than 500 from the Fifteenth Air Force attacked the German targets during the period of February 20 to February 25, 1944; that these bombers dropped an approximate total of 10,000 tons of bombs, which just about equalled the tons of bombs dropped by the Eighth Air Force during its entire first year of operations; and that the cost had been high in both crews and aircraft but not as high as Doolittle had expected.

The general had been braced to accept a loss rate as high as 200 bombers per day during Big Week, but fortunately the total loss figured out to about six percent of the entire force used during the missions—much lower than predicted before the start of the operation. No accurate figures were compiled of men lost on the series of missions, but it is estimated that 2,600 were killed in action, missing, or seriously wounded. In addition approximately

2,500 fighter sorties were flown in support of the Eighth Air Force, with nearly 500 more sorties flown escorting the Fifteenth Air Force bombers from Italy. Only twenty-eight fighters were lost to enemy action.

While there is little controversy over these figures, when an attempt is made to analyze the effect Big Week had on the Luftwaffe and the German aircraft industry, the proponents of air power differ strongly with the opponents of air power. There are many reasons for this difference of opinion.

Opponents of air power, such as John Kenneth Galbraith, attempt to downgrade the efforts of Doolittle's Eighth Air Force as "minor raids that did little to reduce or contain German fighter production." This is an extreme view that can easily be refuted by the events of March, April, May, and June, 1944, when the Eighth Air Force had complete air superiority over the Continent and when the Luftwaffe "only managed minor raids that did little to hamper the Allied cross-Channel invasion," to paraphrase Galbraith. He and others who support his theory base their opinion on the figures compiled after World War II by the US Strategic Bombing Survey, from German records of German fighter production in 1944. These figures indicated that enemy production actually increased after the raids of Big Week, not decreased. The following table was listed by the US Strategic Bombing Survey:

Single Engine Acceptances

1944	
January	1,315
February	1,016
March	1,377
April	1,696
May	1,907
June	2,177

July	2,627
August	2,779

These figures give apparent support to the Galbraith theory, except that a document discovered at Berchtesgaden, an official document with a high-security classification, gives a different analysis of the totals. This document, *Auswertung der Einsatzbereitsch der fliegenden Verb. vom 1 August 1943 bis November 1944,* indicates that a large percentage of the aircraft listed by the US Strategic Bomber Survey were not newly constructed fighters but battle-damaged Luftwaffe aircraft that had been repaired! The German document figures for the same months as those listed in the US Strategic Bombing Survey states:

Fighters of the Jagd Type

1944

	Newly built	Repaired
January	1,162	237
February	794	320
March	934	373
April	1,016	456
May	1,380	384
June	1,704	596
July	1,875	671
August	1,798	676

The total of the German listing compares very closely with the monthly totals of the US Strategic Bombing Survey, so it is fairly certain that repaired German aircraft were included in the American list as "new" fighters.

Another factor pointed out by W.W. Rostow, who supports that theory that Big Week was a decisive factor in the success of the cross-Channel invasion, is that the figures of both the German document and the US Strategic Bombing survey may be misleading. There is no evidence that the planes produced in 1944 were ever delivered to the Luftwaffe, and certainly the operational efficiency of the German Air Force after Big Week didn't reflect any such large increases in its capacity. In fact German records indicate that Luftflotte Reich, the German Air Force command concerned with defending Germany against American heavy bombers, received the following number of single-engine fighters:

Luftflotte Reich

Single-engine acceptances

1944

June	757
July	524
August	439

It is obvious that only a small percentage of the supposedly produced German single-engine fighters were ever delivered to active Luftwaffe units engaged in defending the Reich from Eighth and Fifteenth Air Force bombers.

One answer to this contradictory analysis is the fact that the German Air Force lost many of its best pilots during Big Week and there were no replacements to fly the new aircraft even if they were delivered. While an exact number of pilots lost during this period is not available, a report issued by Galland in the summer of 1944 stated: "Between January and April, 1944, our daytime fighters lost over 1,000 pilots. They included our best squadron,

Gruppe and Geschwader commanders. Each incursion of the enemy is costing us some fifty aircrew. The time has come when our weapon is in sight of collapse."

The losses were due not only to the excellent American pilots flying the long-range escort fighters but the tenacity and accuracy of the gunners aboard the bombers. While the American gunners usually claimed more "kills" than were actually made, because of confusion during the violent air battles and the duplication of claims, German records provide the evidence that refutes those who believed the Luftwaffe was not defeated during Big Week. If it was not completely destroyed and occasionally showed bursts of energy after February, 1944, the threat to the impending cross-Channel invasion by the German Air Force was eliminated.

Many are convinced that the air battles of Big Week during which so many Luftwaffe pilots and planes were lost, were more important than the bombing of the aircraft factories, which were the prime target of the operation. However, this is not entirely true. The bombings of Big Week created a crisis that precipitated a complete reorganization of German aircraft production.

On February 23, 1944, Albert Speer, Hitler's Minister for Armaments, was visited in his sick room by Erhard Milch, Deputy Air Minister under Göring, and was told that the Eighth and Fifteenth Air Forces were concentrating their attacks on the German aircraft industry. Already, according to Milch, production had been reduced to a third of what it had been and something had to be done immediately. During the meeting it was decided that Speer would take over the responsibility of aircraft production despite Göring's objections, and he agreed.

He appointed Karl Saur to handle the job and immediately ordered dispersal of the aircraft production facilities so they would be more difficult to attack. While the dispersal theory proved successful in the long run for the

Germans, it had the indirect effect of causing a loss of aircraft production at the exact moment it was needed most, if the Allied invasion were to be halted. The dispersal of the production facilities also left the German industry dependent on transportation units, which themselves were extremely vulnerable to American heavy bombers. Later attacks on these transportation facilities after the dispersal, forced by Big Week, was completed contributed greatly to the final complete breakdown of the German aircraft industry.

The success of Big Week was never more evident than in the bombing attacks made by the Eighth Air Force and the Fifteenth Air Force during the weeks after the operation ended and the Allied invasion began. On March 4, 1944, the Eighth Air Force bombed Berlin, Hitler's capital, for the first time. The attack on Berlin implied the confidence that Doolittle had in the capability of his heavy bombers to bomb any target on the Continent within range. During the month of March the Eighth Air Force attacked Berlin five times, marking a turning point in the air war. It became obvious during March, one month after Big Week, that the Luftwaffe had lost its superiority over the Continent; and from this time on the rate of loss to enemy aircraft suffered by Doolittle's forces tended to decline sharply.

Besides the damaging attacks on Hitler's capital, the American heavy bombers, in the time left them before the invasion, bombed and in many cases obliterated previously untouched strong points of the German war industry, such as radar, light alloys and chemical plants making highly concentrated hydrogen peroxide for jet fuel. Later the Eighth and Fifteenth Air Force ranged over Europe seeking out and destroying the oil refineries, which ultimately put a halt to the German armies and air units when supplies were depleted.

As Speer told a friend: "I could see the omen of the

war's end when I lay in my sick bed and watched the bombers of the American Fifteenth Air Force fly across the Alps from their Italian bases to bomb German industrial targets and there wasn't a German fighter plane anywhere in sight."

There is no better testimonial to the success of Big Week!

No one knew better than Adolf Galland the havoc the American heavy bombers of Doolittle had wreaked on the German Air Force and the German aircraft industry during Big Week. He watched helplessly as the B-17s and B-24s attacked the oil refineries, the V-weapon sites, the chemical plants, and even Berlin. Now and then he managed to mass enough Luftwaffe fighters to make a serious defense of a target, but these instances became fewer and fewer as the weeks passed after February, 1944. He anticipated that the Allies were planning an invasion of the Continent but there was little he could do about it. The Luftwaffe fighter arm was not in a position to stop the Allied planes that were softening up the area in preparation for the landing. His Number 3 Division was down to eighty to one hundred fighters, while the total Luftwaffe aircraft available on all fronts, according to Galland, was 3,200—of which only about forty percent were in service.

When the Allied landing began on June 6, 1944, he tried to transfer his homeland fighter-defense units to the invasion area, but there were too few, they were too late, and their rate of loss was too high. For several days there was chaos, after that it was defeat by the American fighter pilots.

Galland's forces fought what he called a "jungle warfare" against the Allied air units. Everytime one of his fighters was pushed from a camouflaged hangar in preparation for takeoff, an American fighter roared in and shot it to pieces. After he moved his squadrons into the forests, the American heavy bombers laid a carpet of high explosives over the suspected area and destroyed his planes. The Luftwaffe fighters that did manage to get into the air were outnumbered and usually shot down quickly. Sometimes the German pilot survived, sometimes he died. Within two weeks after the Allied invasion began on June 6, 1944, there were practically no German Air Force attacks on the invading troops.

Galland decided it would be best to withdraw his remaining squadrons to the Reich, reequip them is possible, give them some rest, and replace the empty slots on the personnel roster with some newly trained fliers. He made one serious error, however. He believed that after the Allied invasion began, Doolittle would use his Eighth Air Force aircraft to support the ground troops along the front and forego further strategic bombing of targets deep in Germany.

The American general, however, insisted that the bombing of Germany should continue and Eisenhower agreed. This was the last tragedy for Galland's fighter arm. Against the large-scale bomber raids of the Eighth Air Force, the remnants of the Luftwaffe were powerless. Except for isolated instances when his fighters scored a large number of victories against the bomber formations and its final outburst of energy during the Battle of the Bulge, Galland's fighter arm was finished as an effective combat force.

In January, 1945, a meeting was held in the Haus der Flieger in Berlin while Galland was on leave and many of his proposals and complaints were discussed by Luftwaffe officers who agreed with his theories. Göring, who conducted the meeting, was furious as he heard these officers suggest that the German bomber command had too much influence on the fighter arm, that the jet fighter Me-262 should be used to defend against American bomber attacks instead of as an offensive bomber for the Luftwaffe, and other facts that Galland had been emphasizing for months against Göring's wishes. The following day Galland was summoned to see the Chief of Personnel and told that Göring suspected him of mutiny and that he was dismissed as General of the Fighter Arm and ordered to leave Berlin immediately!

During the last weeks of the war Galland was given a chance to form an elite jet-fighter unit, which was equipped with the Me-262 and was completely independent of all other Luftwaffe units. The official designation of the squadron was JV 44, but it was better known as the "Squadron of Experts." Despite Galland's efforts, however, it was too late for his unit of jet aircraft to have a decisive effect on the outcome of the war.

On April 26, 1944, he led JV 44 on his last mission of World War II, an attack against a formation of American Marauders in the area of Neuburg. It very nearly ended the career of Adolf Galland forever. While shooting down one bomber and making a pass on another, Galland's jet fighter was bounced by a Mustang pilot. The Me-262 was badly damaged and Galland was shot in the knee. Using his long experience and excellent piloting ability, he managed to made a forced landing on a German airfield that was under attack by American planes. He was evacuated from the jet by an armored car and taken to a bomb shelter before he was killed. Later he was removed to a hospital in Munich for treatment of his wound.

It was his last piece of the action. As a brilliant general of the Fighter Arm, he had challenged Doolittle and lost. As commander of an elite jet-fighter unit, he had challenged the American bombers and Mustangs and had lost, again. It was an ignominious end to the fighting for one of the most intelligent and courageous of the Luftwaffe leaders.

"Jimmy" Doolittle and his Eighth Air Force, after gaining air superiority over the German Air Force during Big Week, continued to make deep penetrations into the

Reich, attacking targets that, prior to Big Week, had been considered inaccessible. His predictions had been proven correct, his strategy found successul, his courage and enthusiasm discovered to be more than sufficient to lead the Eighth Air Force to victory over the Luftwaffe, despite every effort Galland and his fighters made to halt the heavy bombers. He directed the operations against the German-controlled oil refineries; sent his Eighth Air Force bombers to attack the V-weapon sites in Operation Crossbow; provided air support for the underground during Operation Carpetbagger; scheduled tactical missions to help the ground troops during Operation Overlord, the Allied invasion of Europe; directed his units of the Eighth Air Force that were involved in Operation Frantic, the shuttle missions to Russia; supported the Allied ground troops in every manner possible during the Battle of the Bulge; and challenged and defeated the Me-262 jet fighters that Galland as General of the Fighter Arm had wanted for his fighter units but had been unable to convince Hitler of their worth until the closing days of the war.

By April, 1945, the Eighth Air Force was running out of targets, and official priorities now amounted to very little. On April 16, 1945, Spaatz sent the following message to Doolittle from his headquarters at Reims:

The advances of our ground forces have brought to a close the strategic air war waged by the United States Strategic Air Forces and the Royal Air Force Bomber Command. It has been won with a decisiveness becoming increasingly evident as our armies overrun Germany.

From now onward our Strategic Air Forces must operate with out Tactical Air Forces in close cooperation with our Armies.

All units of the United States Strategic Air Forces are commended for their part in winning the strategic air war and are enjoined to continue with undiminished effort and precision the final tactical phase of air action to secure the ultimate objective—complete defeat of Germany.

The above is order of the day number 2 and is to be released by this headquarters at 2200 hours tonight.

The strategic air war was ended! Doolittle and his Eighth Air Force had destroyed the capability of Galland's Luftwaffe fighters in a campaign that had reached its climax during Big Week in February, 1944.

The most eloquent testimony to the success of Big Week were the words spoken by General Dwight D. Eisenhower to the ground troops just prior to the invasion on June 6, 1944:

"If you see fighting aircraft over you, they will be ours."

They were!

BIBLIOGRAPHY

Baumbach, Werner. *The Life and Death of the Luftwaffe*. New York: Coward-Macann, Inc., 1960.

Bekker, Cajus. *The Luftwaffe War Diaries*. New York: Doubleday & Company, Inc., 1968.

Caidin, Martin. *Black Thursday*. New York: E.P. Dutton & Co., Inc., 1960. *Forked-Tailed Devil: The P38*. New York: Ballantine Books, Inc., 1971.

Craven, Wesley Frank and Cate, James Lea, eds. *The Army Air Forces in World War II, Volume II: Torch to Pointblank*. Chicago: University of Chicago Press, 1949. *The Army Air Forces in World War II, Volume III: Argument to V-E Day*. Chicago: University of Chicago Press, 1951. *The Army Air Forces in World War II, Volume VII: Services Around the World*. Chicago: University of Chicago Press, 1958.

Deichmann, Paul. *German Air Force Operations in Support of the Army*. New York: Arno Press, 1962.

Dugan, James and Stewart, Carroll. *Ploesti: The Great Ground-Air Battle of 1 August 1943*. New York: Random House, Inc., 1962.

Dupre, Flint O. *U.S. Air Force Biographical Dictionary*. New York: Franklin Watts, Inc., 1965.

Forsberg, Franklin S. *The Best From* Yank *The Army Weekly*. New York: E.P. Dutton & Co., Inc., 1945.

Freeman, Roger A. *The Mighty Eighth: Units, Men and Machines*. New York: Doubleday & Company, Inc., 1970.

Frischauer, Willi. *The Rise and Fall of Hermann Goering*. New York: Ballantine Books, Inc., 1951.

Galland, Adolf. *The First and the Last*. Henry Holt and Company, Inc., 1954.

Glines, Carroll V. *Doolittle's Tokyo Raiders*. Princeton: D. Van Nostrand Company, Inc., 1964.

Green, William. *Famous Bombers of the Second World War*. New York: Hanover House, 1959.

Gurney, Gene. *The War In The Air*. New York: Crown Publishers, Inc., 1962.

Heilmann, Willi. *I Fought You From the Skies*. New York: Award Books, 1966.

Henderson, David B. *The 95th Bombardment Group H*. Cincinnati: A.H. Pugh Printing Co., 1945.

Jablonski, Edward. *Flying Fortress: The Illustrated Biography of the B-17s and the Men Who Flew Them*. New York: Doubleday & Company, Inc., 1965.

Johnen, Wilhelm. *Battling the Bombers*. New York: Ace Books, Inc., 1958.

Killen, John. *A History of the Luftwaffe, 1915–1945*. New York: Doubleday & Company, Inc., 1967.

Knoke, Heinz. *I flew For The Führer*. New York: Henry Holt and Company, Inc., 1953.

LeMay, Curtis E., with Kantor, MacKinlay. *Mission With LeMay*. New York: Doubleday & Company, Inc., 1965.

Leverkuehn, Paul. *German Military Intelligence*. New York: Frederick A. Praeger, Inc., 1954.

Lochner, Louis P., ed. *The Goebbels Diaries*. New York: Doubleday & Company, Inc., 1948.

Loosbrock, John F., ed. and Skinner, Richard M., ed. *The Wild Blue*. New York: G.P. Putnam's Sons, 1961.

Manvell, Roger advised by Franenkel, Heinrich. *Göring*. New York: Ballantine Books, Inc., 1972.

Maurer, Maurer, ed. *Air Force Combat Units of World War II*. Washington: US Government Printing Office, 1960.

Nielsen, Andreas. *The German Air Force General Staff*. New York: Arno Press, 1959.

Peaslee, Budd J. *Heritage of Valor*. New York: J.B. Lippincott Company, 1964.

Price, Alfred. *Pictorial History of the Luftwaffe*. London: Ian Allan, Ltd., 1969.

Rudel, Hans Ulrich. *Stuka Pilot*. New York: Ballantine Books, Inc., 1958.

Speer, Albert. *Inside the Third Reich*. New York: The Macmillan Company, 1970.

Toliver, Raymond F. and Constable, Trevor. *Fighter Aces*. New York: The Macmillan Company, 1965.

Verrier, Anthony. *The Bomber Offensive*. New York: The Macmillan Company, 1969.

INDEX

214

215

216

217

TOP SELLING
World War II
Documentaries & Narratives

IMPERIAL TRAGEDY, by Thomas M. Coffey. The true story of the first and last days of World War II, seen entirely from Japanese eyes. A battle tale, a diplomatic narrative, a study of Japanese society and culture—it is popular history in the best sense of the term—accurate, interesting and lively. From personal interviews given the author by people on all levels of Japanese life who were, somehow, involved in the attack on Pearl Harbor and in the atomic bombing of Hiroshima and Nagasaki. **P00050—$1.95**

BURN AFTER READING, by Ladislas Farago. Here are the spymasters, the heroes, the traitors, and all the cryptic subtlety and horrific violence that marked their grim activities. The more gripping because it really happened—it's all fascinating, particularly if you bear in mind that the same sort of thing is going on right this minute, as clandestinely and just as ruthlessly. By the author of GAME OF THE FOXES and PATTON. Fast-moving, smoothly written, yet fully documented. **P00090—95¢**

THE CANARIS CONSPIRACY, by Roger Manvell and Heinrich Fraenkel. An astounding chronicle of the plot to kill Hitler. This is the documented story of the work of Admiral Wilhelm Canaris' Department Z, pieced together from the accounts of survivors and told in full for the first time. This group attempted to liquidate Hitler in order to make peace with the allies, but before the plotters could achieve their goal, the conspiracy was discovered and broken by arrests, executions and suicides. One of the most incredible stories to come out of World War II. **P00093—$1.25**

DIVINE THUNDER, by Bernard Millot. This is the story of the kamikazes, the suicide pilots of Japan during World War II, and of why, when the need arose, they were ready to die without hesitation. In both soldiers and civilians, a mystical reverence for the homeland was almost second nature. The author describes their devastating assaults and the American reaction to them and he reveals what made the kamikazes men of such strange grandeur and heroism. With original drawings. **P00108—$1.25**

THE MOST POPULAR AND BESTSELLING NON-FICTION FROM PINNACLE BOOKS

BURN AFTER READING, by Ladislas Farago. Here are the spymasters, the heroes, the traitors, and all the cryptic subtlety and horrific violence that marked their grim activities. The more gripping because it really happened—it's all fascinating, particularly if you bear in mind that the same sort of thing is going on right this minute, as clandestinely and just as ruthlessly. By the author of GAME OF THE FOXES and PATTON. Fast-moving, smoothly written, yet fully documented.

P00090-1—95¢

THE CANARIS CONSPIRACY, by Roger Manvell and Heinrich Fraenkel. An astounding chronicle of the plot to kill Hitler. This is the documented story of the work of Admiral Wilhelm Canaris' Department Z, pieced together from the accounts of survivors and told in full for the first time. This group attempted to liquidate Hitler in order to make peace with the allies, but before the plotters could achieve their goal, the conspiracy was discovered and broken by arrests, executions and suicides. One of the most incredible stories to come out of World War II.

P00093-6—$1.25

DIVINE THUNDER, by Bernard Millot. This is the story of the kamikazes, the suicide pilots of Japan during World War II, and of why, when the need arose, they were ready to die without hesitation. In both soldiers and civilians, a mystical reverence for the homeland was almost second nature. The author describes their devastating assaults and the American reaction to them and he reveals what made the kamikazes men of such strange grandeur and heroism. With original drawings.

P00108-8—$1.25

THE KENNEDY WOMEN, by Pearl S. Buck. Here are the fascinating and extraordinary women of the Kennedy family. With the skill of a journalist, the artistry of a gifted storyteller, and the seasoned eye of a biographer, Pearl S. Buck paints a portrait in words of the women who bear one of the most famous family names in history. From Rose, the durable and dynamic matriarch, to JFK's young Caroline—and including Kathleen, Rosemary, Patricia, Jean, Eunice, Ethel, Joan and Jacqueline—these are the ladies of our times.

P00113-4—$1.50

To order see page 224

STAND BY TO DIE, by A. V. Sellwood. The heroic story of a lone, embattled WW II ship. It was a small Yangtse river steamer, manned by a makeshift crew of fugitives. She sailed from war-torn Singapore to do battle with the armed might of a Japanese fleet. It was an epic naval action. Heroism was the order of the day. There were no lean British cruisers to divert the Japanese guns, there were no RAF planes to provide air cover. Just one bullet-riddled tub that wouldn't say die! The story could have been lost forever, as it has been for many years, had not A. V. Sellwood pieced together the almost unbelievable story of "the most decorated small ship in the navy." P00171-1—95¢

SIEGE AND SURVIVAL: THE ODYSSEY OF A LENINGRADER, by Elena Skrjabina. A diary of one of the most devastating sieges in history. During the siege of Leningrad which began on September 8, 1941, nearly one-and-one-half million people died—of hunger, of cold, of disease, from German bullets and bombs. Elena Skrjabina survived. She endured. This book is a record of that experience, and it has been acclaimed by critics everywhere. *Publishers Weekly* said that it is "written in unadorned but eloquent prose that is remarkably effecting." *Bestsellers* said "It is human." P00199-1—95¢

VIZZINI!, by Sal Vizzini, with Oscar Fraley and Marshall Smith. The secret lives of our most successful narc! Sal Vizzini may die because he wrote this book. He was formerly an undercover agent for the Federal Bureau of Narcotics—an assignment which took him to Naples, where he became a "friend" of exiled Mafia chieftain Charles "Lucky" Luciano; to Burma, where he blew up a heroin factory; to Lebanon, where he outwitted a Communist gun-running ring; and to Atlanta, Georgia, where he posed as a con in the Federal pen. He was shot three times, knifed twice, beaten nearly to death, and had several contracts put out by the Mafia to kill him. Many of the men now in jail will learn for the first time who put them there. P00226-2—$1.25

WALKING TALL, by Doug Warren. The true story of Buford Pusser a sheriff who has become a living legend. Buford is an honest man, a good man, he has tried to clean out the criminal element of his community. In doing so he has been shot eight times, stabbed five, rammed by a speeding car, had his home fire bombed, and was trapped in an ambush that killed his wife. But, Buford still lives. He raided the prostitution houses, the gambling dens and illicit moonshine stills and almost single handedly ousted crooked officials. His story has been made into a major motion picture by Cinerama. P00243-2—95¢

To order see page 224

To order see page 224

This is your Order Form . . .
Just clip and mail.

____P00090-1	BURN AFTER READING, Ladislas Farago	.95
____P00093-6	THE CANARIS CONSPIRACY, Manvell & Fraenkel	1.25
____P00108-8	DIVINE THUNDER, Bernard Millot	1.25
____P00113-4	THE KENNEDY WOMEN, Pearl S. Buck	1.50
____P00171-1	STAND BY TO DIE, A. V. Sellwood	.95
____P00199-1	SIEGE & SURVIVAL, Elena Skrjabina	.95
____P00226-2	VIZZINI, Sal Vizzini, with Fraley & Smith	1.25
____P00243-2	WALKING TALL, Doug Warren	.95
____P00244-0	BUGSY, George Carpozi, Jr.	1.25
____P00257-2	MICKEY COHEN: MOBSTER, Ed Reid	1.25
____P00276-9	SUSAN HAYWARD: THE DIVINE BITCH, Doug McClelland	1.25
____P00277-7	INSIDE ADOLF HITLER, Manvell & Fraenkel	1.50

TO ORDER

Please check the space next to the book/s you want, send this order form together with your check or money order, include the price of the book/s and 15¢ for handling and mailing, to:

PINNACLE BOOKS, INC. / P.O. Box 4347, Grand Central Station / New York, N.Y. 10017

☐ **CHECK HERE IF YOU WANT A FREE CATALOG.**

I have enclosed $_____ check_____ or money order_____ as payment in full. No C.O.D.'s.

Name_____

Address_____

City_____ State_____ Zip_____
(Please allow time for delivery.)